FORWARD

To win, you must know how to play the game.

Unfortunately, the rules and tactics that winners consistently use in the game of life have not been written down in one place for all to study. Until now.

Success in life is not unlike the dilemma faced in your first job interview. Do you remember the challenge? Getting the job seemed to require "relevant experience." But how were you to acquire it without having that first job? Life's like that too. Success is largely dependent on learning some things that people never tell you.

Which is precisely why this book will interest you. If you want to play the game more expertly and increase your winning percentage, this book will certainly give you a competitive advantage. Of course, it will tell you some things you already know. But it will also tell you a few things, about yourself as well as the other players in the game, that you likely haven't considered. And that's what's important. In life, it's what you don't know that can hurt you.

The Game of Life shows you how to overcome the frustrating and debilitating effects of dealing with puzzling and challenging people. It demonstrates how to take control of difficult situations. It provides practical strategies for turning conflict into cooperation. It outlines the process, skills, tactics and guiding principles that each of us can use to prevent tension and turmoil in significant relationships. It tells you how to master the game and thereby enhance the quality of your life.

Which is what winning is all about.

ACKNOWLEDGEMENTS

It is said that we all stand on someone else's shoulders. That is an apt description of *The Game of Life*. Dale Carnegie, who apparently took 25 years of his life to write an earlier book about winning the game, perhaps said it best: "The ideas I stand for are not mine. I borrowed them from Socrates. I swiped them from Chesterfield. I stole them from Jesus. And I put them in a book. If you don't like their rules, whose would you use?"

I am indebted to many writers and researchers for their insights, theories and war stories. I have stumbled, crawled and raced through their findings in my quest for answers about our common pursuit of coexistence while fulfilling personal needs and aspirations. I have had the privilege of meeting many seminal thinkers personally—to challenge them, as they did me. Among these fellow travellers are: Robert Bramson, who may have pioneered the notion of "difficult people"; Herb Cohen, whose wit and practical knowledge enriched my teaching; Gerard Nierenberg, for his focus on the critical importance of needs; Deborah Tannen, Suzette Hayden Elgin and Anne Ruhl for their thoughts on gender differences. Not surprisingly, this list goes on.

Like most writers on this timeless topic, I have borrowed ideas from many but have assembled them in a unique and hopefully provocative way. Like assembling a jig-saw puzzle, I have taken some old pieces, added in new ones and configured them into my peculiar view of the game of life, its guiding principles and what it takes to play the game intelligently and with sensitivity.

Naturally, there are acknowledgements of a more personal nature. Important people who have contributed much to my learning the game along the way. People who tolerated my unrelenting inquiry into why we behave as we do. People whom my ideas have occasionally annoyed. And good friends who had the patience and grace to indulge me these notions and the courage to tell me when they thought I was crazy. Special people about whom I care greatly. Fortunately, they know who they are.

Lastly, I am indebted to my editor, colleague and spouse...she holds up the mirror daily and reminds me why we play the game.

NOTES

On Simplicity: Despite the obvious scope of this topic, a concerted effort has been made to ensure simplicity. The use of technical jargon has been kept to a minimum. For ease of reading, there are no footnotes and, despite a vast literature, a bibliography has not been included. For the more devoted reader, a listing of resource materials may be found on the companion Internet web site (*www.the-game-of-life.com*).

On Gender: Constant reference to *he* and *she* (and derivatives thereof), if grammatical correctness is to be maintained, can make reading awkward. I acknowledge that both women and men are players in the game; that is why reference is frequently made to both genders. However, a conscious effort has been made to avoid such communication atrocities as: "Since he or she is incapable of evaluating the consequences of his (her) behaviour, your primary objective is to get him/her to regain his/her composure."

On Inferring Reality: As is customary in works of this kind, the reader must neither assume nor infer that real people or events have been used to illustrate key points, although the game situations depicted might appear familiar. The illustrations and advice offered reflect the personal opinions and observations of the author by virtue of his research, unique experiences and expertise. All examples are used for illustrative purposes only and are therefore not factual. Any characterizations, names ascribed or descriptions made of either people or events that might appear to resemble real situations or individuals are wholly unintentional.

✧ THE GAME

Life is not a game.

On analysis, the analogy cannot be sustained. Games are, by definition, competitive. Life need not be. Cooperation, collaboration and mutual profit improvement are preferable to competing. In a game, we compete to win. Therefore, it follows, I can only win at your expense. Yet, in life, it is possible for both of us to win. And, once we know how, we can do so consistently.

Games encompass a finite number of variables. Yet life is surely infinite in its variability. Constant change, unforeseen circumstances, personal growth and new information ensure not only life's variability but also its unpredictability.

If life is not a game, why do we persist in calling it one? We do so because it is a useful metaphor for understanding the complexities of life and making it slightly less intimidating. The purpose of models, analogies and allegories, after all, is to help make simple and more intelligible the complicated and intricate. Which is what life is, most of the time.

Seeing life as a game can be helpful. It can provide us with much needed perspective and "emotional distance" from demanding people, tough choices and difficult situations. That's because games are not real. They are less frightening than reality and they are typically fun to play. Moreover, when we play, we usually focus our attention on what it takes to "win," however we might choose to define that term. That objective is the primary focus of the serious player, the one who is committed to winning consistently.

That is my purpose in writing this book—to help you learn how to focus your attention on what it takes to win the game of life.

There is ample evidence to suggest that, perhaps, life is a game. Eugene Hare, for example, once observed that "Life is like a game of whist. From unseen sources the cards are shuffled, and the hands are dealt." It's an interesting and instructive point of view. It suggests we not waste time debating our circumstances but rather focus our attention and skills on making the most of them. Josh Billings added his contribution to the life-as-a-card-game metaphor when he said "Life consists not in holding the cards but in playing those you hold well." And Kenny Rogers, as the aging gambler, once observed that "You've got to know when to hold them and know when to fold them." Such analogies offer us important insights and sound wisdom

11

for dealing more effectively with life's challenges and complexities.

These metaphors help us to explain what life is all about. Here are others for your reflection—some literary, some musical, some philosophical, some downright earthy:

> "Life is something like a trumpet. If you don't put anything in, you won't get anything out."   (W.C. Handy)

> "Life is like playing a violin solo in public and learning the instrument as one goes on."   (Samuel Butler)

> "Life is a banquet, and some poor sons of bitches are starving." (Auntie Mame)

> "Life is an onion. You peel it off one layer at a time and sometimes you weep."
>   (Carl Sandburg)

> "Life is like eating artichokes. You've got to go through so much to get so little."
>   (T.A. Dorgan)

If life can be "a scrambled egg" (Don Marquis), "a spaceship" (Buckminster Fuller), "a B-picture script" (Kirk Douglas) or "a cabaret" (Liza Minnelli), surely it can also be "a game."

But if you are to treat life as a game, what are its objectives? Doubtless you can think of many—some noble, some utopian, some entirely personal and self-serving. Whatever your purpose in life, the objective must surely be to achieve it at minimal expense, disruption or harm to yourself and others. But that success is impossible unless others—especially those who oppose your goal—can eventually agree with your point of view and with your rules for playing the game.

Isn't it possible that the real purpose of the game is to get others to agree with you? Minimally, you must get others to change their point of view so as not to oppose yours. Ultimately, you seek to ensure that others will see things your way, with the way that things *should* be.

Whatever you do in life, whether you're selling or buying something, persuading superiors or motivating subordinates, whether your focus is on parent-child or spousal relationships, complex business dealings or management-labour relations, your primary objective is to get others to align with your view and eventually concur. That accomplishment is central to your ability to satisfy your needs, exchange ideas, change attitudes, improve relationships and influence behaviour.

Despite its importance to your happiness and the quality of your existence, your ability to influence others is largely a function of trial and error. Unfortunately, the subject is not taught in schools, though some of us do benefit from parents or mentors who can translate their wisdom about life in meaningful ways. From them, we discover that the capacity to change the viewpoints of others is really a skill as much as an attitude. From them, we learn that our ability to influence the thinking and the behaviour of others can determine the outcome of complex social and business relationships, as well as immeasurably enhance the quality of our own lives.

Those who lack such wise counsel in their formative years must discover how to play the game on their own. They must learn from their own successes and failures, provided they be conscientious learners. While experience is an effective teacher, it means we acquire the insight too late to enable us to seize meaningful opportunities as they arise. Moreover, consciously or not, those we encounter in the game are using their own time-tested tactics to influence our behaviour, our choices and our decisions.

Our inability or inexperience in recognizing these manipulations, as well as our own uncertainty or ineptness in using appropriate countermeasures, does affect our personal and organizational success. Without the requisite know-how, a knowledge of the game's rules and the tactics of the other players, we are more likely to lose in our encounters with players who are more skilled in the game.

This book can give you a real advantage in the game of life. Although I am not a psychologist, I have spent most of my adult life studying human behaviour and, more specifically, our capacity for solving problems and satisfying needs. I have communicated my discoveries through my teaching and writing. Almost 300,000 people from all walks of life have attended a variety of life skills courses which I developed over the past two decades. They include such topics as The Creative Genius Within, The Art of Negotiating...with anyone, Conflict Management, Change by Choice, Transformational Thinking, and The Subtle Art of Influencing Difficult People. For 10 years, I wrote a magazine column, entitled "The People Puzzle", which focused on these same topics and the game's seemingly unending challenges.

Not surprisingly, *The Game of Life* encapsulates much of this research and teaching. These are my observations on the dynamics of human behaviour in conflict situations, whether at the breakfast table, in the office or at the bargaining table. The guidelines, tactics and insights offered in these pages will not only help you better understand "the games people play" but also your own emotions as these games unfold. The more you utilize the suggestions outlined, the more you will discover how to benefit from human nature rather than continuing to fight it. You will learn how to take back control of your relationships. And you will appreciate how to create opportunities to get your work done without undue frustration, anger and confusion.

Surely the ultimate goal in the game of life is the realization of more productive and harmonious relationships and the satisfaction of your personal, professional and organizational needs. With proper execution and continued refinement, you can discover how to solve your people puzzles, turn conflict into cooperation and appreciably reduce the anxiety and uncertainty in your life.

LEARNING ABOUT LIFE

To be a successful player in the game, you must become a discerning learner. Despite what some might think, adults can be good learners. The trick, to call it that, lies not so much in learning new things but in unlearning unproductive habits. Success requires that we rid ourselves of unthinking responses, of ideas and techniques that no longer "work" in influencing others. Those who think they cannot learn a better way to achieve their objectives will never be serious players in the game of life. Rather, they are destined to become its unwitting victims.

Learning, for me, is making a meaningful connection between someone else's ideas and my reality. Learning rarely occurs in the classroom nor does it emanate from books or the wisdom of those with more experience. Rather, it is only when I discover for myself the relevance, utility and meaning of the idea for my life that I have truly learned something.

Certainly the insights which I find to be beneficial often originate with those same reliable sources—teachers, experts, authors, journalists, philosophers, anthropologists, theologians, etc. But it is I who must decide what is the best or the most useful concept for me in the context of *my* life. Then I must do it. Because, when all is said and done, learning comes from doing. Whether the result of that doing is success or failure, I learn solely as a consequence of my behaviour. If I take the time to reflect on the experience, I will make a meaningful new connection. I will have learned something.

Learning is the acquisition of comfort (knowing why) and competence (knowing how). This symbiotic relationship brings to mind the inconsequential chicken-or-egg conundrum. Which one comes first? That is an unproductive debate. To get better in life, we must have both. One reinforces the other. The more comfortable you feel, the more competently you will perform. As a consequence, the more comfortable (and more artful) you will be when you have to do it again. Learning is continuous.

What I seek to impart to the discerning learner is both comfort and competence in the art of playing the game of life. What you will discover in acquiring this new sense of self-confidence are a few guiding principles (let's call them tools) with which to continue to build your own mastery of the game.

First, you will receive a map of the territory, something that can tell you where you are relative to your destination, something that will outline alternate routes for getting there safely, in the least amount of time and with the least amount of aggravation. This is the "game board". For it is only when you "see" the board clearly that you can fully appreciate, if not understand, your tactical choices and options. Like aerial photography, by rising above the field of play, you can see in all directions. This revealing vantage point provides a distinct advantage in the game.

You will also need to know the basic "rules" of the game. As with all games, this knowledge will help you make better tactical decisions. Not surprisingly, these rules are founded upon the predictable behaviours of people like you and me as we go about our daily pursuits.

Lastly, and perhaps more importantly, you will need to recognize who the other players are, at least the more challenging ones you are likely to encounter en route to your chosen destination. You will want to be armed with appropriate insights and countertactics to negate their favourite gambits. You will need to know what motivates them and how to uncover their weaknesses. You will want to understand how to modify their particularly troublesome behaviours. You will want to know how to win their game.

Plato observed that "without knowledge, we will walk lame to the end of our lives." But knowing the tools and learning how to use them are two entirely different things (to paraphrase another philosopher, Yogi Berra).

Although this book provides the requisite knowledge for playing the game of life, learning how to use that knowledge is what success is all about. It is you who must choose what you need to learn, and what skills and tactics you must adapt to "fit" your unique personality. That strategic choice will determine what you will actually take from these pages. And, in time, this commitment to continuous and conscientious learning may enable you to master the game.

1 THE OBJECT

Conflict is a cooperative process.

Conflict is an inevitable part of daily living. Rarely does a day pass that we don't see it occurring in some way. In personal, social and business affairs, we encounter people in conflict. It is a reality for each of us simply because its primary cause is that people have different perceptions, information, and needs.

What comes to mind when you hear the word *conflict*? If you're like most people, some of the words you think of immediately are: fight, anger, disappointment, frustration, panic, and anxiety. Do you detect the common theme? In word-association tests, people overwhelmingly view conflict in negative terms. They rarely think of the good things we can also associate with the word—like change, growth, creativity, progress and win-win outcomes. The normal tendency is to perceive conflict as something bad and as something that offers us limited and unpleasant choices, like "fight or flee." This mind-set is a primary reason why we invariably are unable to handle challenging people and difficult situations. Negative thoughts are not creative thoughts. Rather, they are incapacitating thoughts.

Our feelings about conflict were imprinted early in life. Can you recall your first encounters with conflict? Perhaps it occurred when your parents lashed out at one another. Maybe you witnessed a close friend being set upon by bullies in the schoolyard. Or it could be as simple as a teacher or parent advising you to "turn the other cheek" whenever conflict arose. Whatever the event, your initial contact with conflict was not a positive experience. And your emotional response towards conflict likely hasn't changed dramatically over the years. Blame it on this early socialization if you will but your attitude towards conflict speaks directly to your ability to deal with it. In learning to fear conflict, we developed feelings and responses that are usually counterproductive to our objectives in conflict situations.

Yet conflict is unavoidable. You can expect more of it in your life, not less. That forecast need not necessarily trouble you, because conflict is inherently neither good nor bad. It simply is. This perspective is crucial to your success in the game of life.

Conflict has the *potential* to be a positive and creative force. Indeed, without it, there rarely can be progress or growth. Conflict can be used for legitimate or illegitimate ends. It can be meaningful or it can be pointless. Intense inner conflict, for example, is often a prelude to emotional and intellectual growth. Ultimately, learning requires conflict. When our precious assumptions are challenged by others or by new

16

circumstances or new information, we typically adapt and learn new things.

How we choose to use conflict is what can make the difference in our lives. An understanding of the nature, causes, and functions of conflict, and what its enormous potential can do for us, is essential to developing new attitudes and skills that will enable us to be better players in the game.

NEGATIVE CONFLICT

Conflict that we are unable to control is negative. It escalates independent of its causes and often continues long after these have become irrelevant or been forgotten. Parallelling this escalation is an increasing reliance on power and the tactics of threat, coercion and deception. As a result, the antagonists move away from attempts to minimize or reconcile differences or enhance mutual understanding.

Negative conflict forces a competition to win at almost any cost. Communication between antagonists is unreliable and impoverished. The enhancement of one's own power at the expense of the other's becomes the prime objective. Ensuing attitudes of suspicion and hostility serve only to increase the sensitivity to differences, while minimizing an awareness of similarities.

Negative conflict is characterized as "win-lose" because the goal is for one person to win at the expense of the other. In such win-lose encounters, the parties have relatively little interest in discovering innovative, constructive solutions that might be acceptable to both sides. Conversely, in a win-win situation, people collaborate with the intent of discovering areas for mutual profit improvement.

The win-lose approach to conflict resolution generally creates a set of dynamics which tends to aggravate the struggle. Over time, these become a fuel driving the parties further apart and encouraging the use of even more aggressive and hostile tactics.

POSITIVE CONFLICT

Conflict can also create wonderful opportunities for cooperative problem solving and the achievement of mutually rewarding outcomes. Clearly, one of the more positive functions of conflict is its ability to arouse the motivation needed to solve a problem that might otherwise go unattended.

Positive conflict promotes open and honest communication as issues are clarified and hidden causes brought to the surface where they can be addressed. It encourages a recognition of the legitimacy of the other's concerns and grievances. And it leads to a trusting attitude that serves to increase the mutual sensitivity to common interests, beliefs, and values.

A cooperative problem-solving process encourages openness and the full use of available resources. Just as competition leads ultimately to misperception and misjudgment, cooperation tends to reduce defensiveness and the perceived differences between people. In place of the tactics of coercion, a strategy of problem solving typically uses persuasion, discovery of needs, openness, and mutual enhancement of interests—an approach that engenders cooperation and enhances perceptions of benevolence. The objective is not to win at all costs but to find common needs that produce acceptable "third options" and creative synergy.

An orientation towards conflict that highlights common needs and defines the conflict as a mutual problem is more likely to take a constructive course towards resolution than an approach that emphasizes antagonistic interests, seeks to maximize power differences, and defines the conflict as a win-lose contest.

Without some tension and conflict in the game, there can be no creativity, adaptation or progress. Almost every creative genius our civilization has produced has experienced conflict or adversity in some aspect of their lives. They confronted disappointments and problems of a physical, social, economic, religious, or political kind. They not only prevailed, they grew and achieved success in the process. They also became extraordinary problem solvers.

In a conflict situation, resolution demands creativity. The objective is to think of innovative ways to overcome the barriers to mutual needs satisfaction.

TURNING CONFLICT INTO COOPERATION

Conflict is "the given" in the game of life. It is neither good nor bad. It's the context for the game's manoeuvres and gambits. It's the "game board"—the field of play upon which our encounters with the other players take place. The object is to use conflict to advantage. Whenever we seek to accomplish our goals, we need to know how to turn negative conflict into positive conflict. We need to know how to turn the unavoidable incidences of conflict into opportunities for cooperation and mutual interest enhancement.

To use conflict to your advantage, however, you must first get it "into the open" where you can understand it. In doing so, you must be receptive to the signals and mixed messages people "give off" which indicate the existence of conflict despite statements they may be making to the contrary.

Whenever you sense there may be difficulty in a relationship, the best approach is the direct approach: *"I get the feeling something's bothering you, Wilma. Is there a problem?"* Whatever the response (some people prefer denial to remedy), if you pay close attention to the signals, you may detect the existence of the problem. In my experience, if you sense the possibility of a problem in the relationship, there usually is one. Your choice is whether you want to address it. And, if so, when and how.

The existence of a problem in the relationship may reveal itself in the immediacy of the reply, in the tone of voice or in the exact words. Any inconsistency in tonality or inflection of voice or any incongruency in the three channels of communication (words, voice tone and body language) could alert you to the existence of a hidden concern.

Let's examine one of Wilma's possible responses to your query. Averting her eyes from you, she quickly replies, *"No, no. It's nothing, really."* Is there a problem here? What's the significance of *"it's"*? Why the added *"really"*? We tend to take people too literally during these encounters. Our normal desire to avoid a conflict often leads us into a state of wishful hearing rather than listening to the actual words spoken or to the feelings behind the words. We think we hear the meaning but we don't make the effort to listen to the tone of the voice or pay attention to possible contradictory body signals.

AIRING CONFLICT

Getting conflict into the open where you can deal with it is a critical skill in the game. It is a process of discovery that demands persistence. *"Wilma, I believe there is a problem and, unless you think it's none of my business, I'd like to know what it is."* You've taken the next step in airing the conflict. Now say no more. Simply wait for her reply. Asking appropriate questions and the patience to listen empathically for the answers are vital to your success. The immediate objective is to "tune in" to her frame of reference, to try to understand how she sees the problem or how she might be feeling about it.

Active listening and reflection skills enable you to handle confrontation effectively and influence the desired behaviour. Active listening is paying careful attention to both the *content* of the message and the *feelings* behind the words. Content is what the words mean; feeling is how the person actually feels about what she is saying (e.g., anger, joy, fear, confusion, frustration, etc.).

Reflection is restating, in your own words, what you understand the other person to have just said. You do not judge, question, argue or evaluate; you simply restate (and thus reflect) the message back to the sender. The purpose of active listening and reflection is to build rapport, show that you understand and care, generate further dialogue, and help to confirm your understanding of what the other person is saying and feeling. It's called quality communication.

THE PROCESS

Like everything else you'll discover in *The Game of Life*, to successfully solve your people puzzles and ultimately win the game, you must follow some basic steps.

These steps, in sequence, constitute what is known as a process. It's a structure—
something you can hold on to when the going gets tough. What follows are the five
sequential steps for resolving a conflict:

1. *Define the conflict.*
2. *Value the person.*
3. *Understand the conflict.*
4. *Select an appropriate response.*
5. *Encourage problem solving.*

Define the conflict. Once the conflict has been "aired," you must determine
whether you are dealing with a disagreement that is borne of either personal values
and perceptions or concrete, substantive issues. Rarely can a conflict over personal
values be resolved. To illustrate, a Catholic is unlikely to convince a devout agnostic
that she is wrong in her beliefs. Nor is the converse probable. These are personal
beliefs that are not easily modified or changed.

Values conflicts can be managed, however. This means keeping the implications and repercussions of the conflict within acceptable bounds. The "value v.s.
issue" determination is a critical initial assessment of what you can and cannot
accomplish. Not every conflict can or will be resolved to everyone's satisfaction. Such
strategic choices are an integral part of the game.

An easy way to separate personal values from concrete issues is to apply *the
consequences test.* Ask yourself, "What are the consequences of Harold's behaviour (or
his beliefs) for me? for the organization? for our relationship? for him? If there are no
specific consequences, the conflict lies solely in how you *feel* about it. The other
person's behaviour (or his beliefs) merely conflict with your values...with the way you
feel it ought to be done. This conflict is unlikely to be resolved unless someone
changes his value bias.

An effective way of moving values conflicts into the issues arena is to operationalize them. Make the values concrete. When you can discuss the appropriateness
of a given behaviour at a particular moment in time, for example, you begin to focus
on the consequences (of the behaviour) rather than on the other's values.

Value the Person. Interdependence and mutuality of interests are essential to
successful conflict resolution. To obtain the information necessary to deal with the
concern at hand, you must know how to value the other person. Valuing draws
people together and encourages cooperation. It enables us to communicate with each
other in a manner that builds credibility, civility, rapport and trust.

If you can't value yourself first, it's unlikely that you will value others. Here are some guidelines for ensuring you are comfortable with your own self-appraisal. You value yourself when:

- *You can decide who you want to be* without making excuses, justifying your behaviour or saying "I'm sorry."

- *You understand that it's your life* and what happens in it is entirely up to you. You set realistic goals and you don't demand perfection from yourself.

- *You refuse to be manipulated* by the greed, helplessness or anger of others. You set limits and say "no" when you mean "no." You stand up for what you think is right.

- *You don't feel a need to be liked* or obligated to answer questions (especially questions that are threatening, demanding or manipulative), if it is contrary to your own best interest.

- *You stay in the "here-and-now"* and cope with reality. If you blame others or the world for all your problems, you are not being realistic. Rather, you are being a victim.

Self-knowledge, the ability to understand and value yourself, is a necessary attribute for success in the game of life. When you possess it, you can more easily value others. Doing so in conflict situations is the foundation for generating win-win outcomes. Here are some simple rules for valuing others:

- *Listen empathically.* Don't think of counterarguments while the other person is presenting his case. Open your mind to possibilities. Walk in the other person's "moccasins" (reasoning).

- *Don't make assumptions* about how others think or feel or how they should react. The only head you can get inside is your own.

- *Don't generalize about feelings* even in a kidding fashion. Don't make sweeping judgments about behaviour (as dumb, lazy or childish) or feelings, especially whether they are real, important or morally right or wrong.

- *Don't be manipulative.* Be honest, direct and specific. Don't correct others' statements about how they are feeling. Don't tell them how they "should" feel.

- *Don't state your opinions as facts.* Avoid preaching. Don't exaggerate or bully others. Give people the benefit of the doubt and the room to move.

- *Involve others in the process* if your decisions will affect them. We have a basic need to feel a part of decisions that affect our lives.

- *Be clear on roles and goals.* Healthy people (and relationships) know where they're going and what they must do in order to get there. Use mutual goals, not personal values or preferences, to test whether issues are relevant or important.

Valuing others creates credibility, trust and the interpersonal dynamics that lead to direct, undistorted, candid and authentic communication. This is the kind of communication that is essential to handling confrontation, influencing others and taking control of the game.

Understand the conflict. When you value people, you create a climate where differences can surface. To understand the nature of a conflict, you must delay your initial tendency to negatively judge ideas, beliefs, feelings, attitudes, behaviour or concerns. Listen actively for both the facts and the feelings. Empathize with their perspective; it is a legitimate point of view for them. Differences of opinion are normal and natural. Learn to value diversity.

A true understanding of conflict requires that you probe its dynamics and dimensions. As in problem solving, the better your definition of the conflict, the easier will be its resolution. Although it may not be a matter of choice, try (to the extent possible) to select problems that you can do something about. And make sure that you are discussing the real problem; it is often too convenient to mask the essence of the difficulty that confronts us.

Once you believe you've stated the conflict as accurately as possible and to the satisfaction of both parties, try to identify the situational factors. What are the problems and opportunities, strengths and weaknesses with which you must contend? Face the hard facts realistically rather than just being nice to each other. Try to avoid linear thinking, tunnel vision and instant-solution focus. If you're in a group setting, depersonalize the problem solving, build cohesiveness and candidly attempt to deal with any hidden agendas. Above all, listen attentively and supportively. It will amaze you how active listening encourages the free and full expression of different points of view.

Select an appropriate response. Your tactics must fit the conflict. The game is about choosing the right response for the circumstance at hand. The skill of influencing others lies in your ability to focus on the specific behaviour and its tangible consequences while, at the same time, not falling prey to the tactics of those whose behaviour offends. This requires developing your self-control and presence of mind (important strengths to be examined more deeply).

This outline of the key steps in the process is not a formula that guarantees success. It is *a structure* that will give you support and direction when you need it. Supplementing these basic steps is an array of tactics and responses that are specific to the player and the situation. Depending on the person and the nature of the encounter, you must ensure your response is appropriate to the game being played. There is no need to bludgeon a weak adversary. It is a waste of time and energy. Over-kill will only prove counterproductive in the long run. It is unethical (and, in a business situation, unprofessional). It is cowardly. And your reputation is at risk. In the game of life, it's shortsighted to create an opportunity for remorse, recrimination or revenge.

Encourage problem solving. This ultimate step is where you eventually want to be in your encounters with other players. It begins with a simple question: "*What do you think we can do about it* (the situation, your behaviour, our problems, etc.)?" Always permit the other person to volunteer her ideas first. Resist the temptation to judge or offer your solutions or opinions first. Practise non-directive listening and list the alternatives and options they provide, without evaluating them. This you can do more readily when all the possibilities have been identified.

Define the criteria and conditions that a solution must meet to be acceptable to both parties. Focus on merits, principles and issues rather than on personal values, perceptions and preferences. Don't create a values conflict in the midst of solution finding. Seek innovate ideas and alternatives by using different frames of reference and creative problem-solving techniques, like brainstorming. Strive for mutually satisfying solutions, those "third options" that ensure a benefit or profit to both sides. It can be done.

A knowledge of conflict dynamics and an understanding of the conflict resolution process will enable you to better understand the object of the game. Which, simply put, is to turn conflict situations into opportunities for cooperation.

2 BARRIERS TO WINNING

Discover your pause button.

Playing the game successfully demands a degree of self-knowledge. This requires you to pay attention to your hot buttons, which the other players are adept at finding and pushing. The ability to manage your hot buttons during the game will significantly reduce the incidence of unproductive conflicts in your life. It will also help you play the game with style and grace.

Hot buttons is a term we use to indicate unthinking, emotional responses. It describes our vulnerabilities—"soft spots" that trigger stress, anger, frustration, confusion, jealousy, guilt, anxiety, depression, fear and other unproductive feelings. These reactions are typically inappropriate or disproportionate to the annoyance, irritation or attack that causes them. Hot buttons are also natural defences against insincere criticism and accusations—tactics often used to gain advantage.

When we react to people, we have a choice. We can react emotionally, in which case our behaviour becomes either offensive or defensive. Alternatively, we can react rationally—thereby enabling a variety of strategic and thus more appropriate responses. Contrary to popular opinion, opposites do not attract. The people we likely find the most difficult to deal with are those who are the least like us. And the people who are least like us are the ones toward whom we tend to react emotionally. Stated another way, our hot buttons become exposed in the presence of people whose personalities are dissimilar to our own.

In developing a hot button immune system, the adage "know thyself" is good advice. Self-knowledge is, in effect, your pause button. This is more than an awareness of your strengths and talents or of attributes that make you feel competent, confident and powerful. Rather, real self-knowledge is knowing your weaknesses, biases and prejudices—the things that make you "human". Knowing those weaknesses, and acknowledging them openly, will make you less vulnerable to taking negative criticism and accusations personally.

KNOW THYSELF

How can you get to know yourself better and, in the process, discover your pause button? To develop insights into your personal strengths and weaknesses, try answering these questions honestly in the context of how you usually deal with people who irritate you:

24

- How do I feel about these people and why do I feel this way?

- Do these feelings help or hinder my efforts to deal with them?

- What are my personal strengths? How can I use them more fully?

- What are my limitations? How can I correct these deficiencies?

- What is my self-image? Is it reasonably accurate?

- Does it impair my efforts to communicate with others?

- What are my prejudices and stereotypes (that lead me to prejudge people without evidence)?

- What are my pet peeves and sacred cows?

- How can I prevent these hot buttons from affecting my game?

- Where am I vulnerable emotionally?

- Does ego-inflating behaviour make me a willing victim?

- What don't I like about myself? Is this reality-based?

- To what extent, and why, do I have the respect of colleagues?

- What prompts them to lessen their respect for me?

- What satisfaction am I really seeking from others? Why?

Finding honest answers to questions such as these will significantly reduce the incidence of unproductive conflict in your life. This awareness alone will enable you to be less vulnerable to those who may be intent on manipulating your feelings. It will permit you to make rational decisions when under attack. And that's what will constitute your success in the game of life—the ability to make strategic choices under pressure.

REDUCING UNPRODUCTIVE CONFLICT

Unproductive conflict is that which is physically, emotionally or socially harmful to one or both parties in the relationship. Here are a few guidelines and suggestions for keeping your involvement in unproductive conflicts to a minimum.

First, it's important to distinguish between your principles and your preferences. Most arguments are about trivial matters—differences of opinion or of perception. Yet we often choose to escalate these disagreements in spite of the consequences, seeing them as contests to be won or lost. But differences of opinion and perception are normal and natural. No two people could ever see anything in precisely the same way. A more constructive perspective is to view these differences as alternatives and opportunities for creativity. When you know your personal priorities and values, you tend to avoid unproductive conflict. You also become more selective in your responses to those who would prefer to argue.

Reality test your expectations of others. Conflict often ensues when we expect more of others than they can give or are willing to give. Learn to accept what is real, not what you think "should" be. Practise the power of optimism in the presence of people whom you value; often *what you think is what you get*. Praise will lead to growth more quickly than will criticism. The challenge with criticism is that people generally don't know how to accept it. Remember, the world is filled with people who feel compelled to tell you about your shortcomings. Reacting to criticism is a hot button.

Unproductive conflicts (and hot button responses) are less likely to occur when you recognize common, everyday situations that irritate you—things like a cluttered or crowded environment, poor time management, excessive "noise" and disruptions, over-commitment to others, poor health and the like. Realize that you are in charge of your life and it is therefore *you* who can choose to avoid most, if not all, of these conflict arousers and traps.

In the presence of people who tend to cause you difficulty, try to suspend your judgment for awhile. We are too quick to "shoot from the lip" when we are wary of or dislike others. It is often the stereotype (the mental image) rather than the person to which we react. Try to develop some "trust credits" by consciously building good will through considerate behaviour. Two relatively easy ways to build trust are listening to others and asking for their help. You can then draw on your "account" whenever it's needed.

Anticipate negative conflict. It happens more easily and more frequently than does positive conflict, so plan for it. How? By recognizing and dealing with conflict situations when they are minor incidents or annoyances, and therefore more manageable. You can prevent an unnecessary escalation of the conflict by sharing information and negotiating your expectations of each other. This reduces the uncertainty and lack of clarity in your relationship goals and roles. It helps you to understand what is expected of each other.

THE BIG BUTTON

"You make me so angry!" "If the kids were better behaved, I wouldn't get so angry!" "It's your fault I feel this way!" "He makes me so mad!" For many players in the game, the most difficult hot button is anger. It is a physically arousing emotion, a survival response, a feeling of intense displeasure that results when we are mis-treated, injured or perceive threat. It is manifest as an urge to fight back at the apparent cause of the feeling. Anger is an important emotion—a signal to which we must pay attention and take seriously in understanding its power over us.

When displayed inappropriately, anger is the primary reason why you lose more often than you win. When dealing with challenging players, in particular, your anger is close to the surface. These players are especially attuned to your hot buttons, much like a shark that senses blood in the water. Not surprisingly, this is a key part of their strategy. They know how to use *your* anger to get what *they* want. When anger immobilizes you, demoralizes you or reduces your credibility, the other player has achieved his objective.

You would be a remarkable human being if you never blamed someone or some incident for your feelings of anger. But neither people nor events *make* you angry. It is your feelings about those people or events that create your anger. Even when a genuinely negative incident occurs, it is the meaning you attach to it that determines your emotional response. Consider the following illustration.

When 16 year old Stephanie talks back to her father, Dick, he seems to roll with it. He is able to deflect her sarcasm and rudeness. He maintains his cool. When she goes too far, he simply suggests she "save" her remarks or he'll end the conver-sation. On the other hand, Marie, Stephanie's mother, is outraged by the smart-aleck attitude. If Stephanie dares to use that tone of voice with her, Marie either grounds her or imposes a sanction: "No phone calls for the rest of the evening". If Stephanie has a comeback comment, Marie is quick to explode and end up, in a shrieking voice, demanding respect. Marie can't understand the new generation. When she was a kid, adults were always treated with respect.

To understand Dick's demeanor is to know that he was raised in a large family where the children were encouraged to be self-reliant. New ideas were welcomed. Signs of increasing independence in each child were accepted and praised. Teenage rebellion, when it happened, was considered normal, an indication that the children were growing up. Dick remembers those years fondly as challenging and fun.

Marie was the elder of two girls. Her parents were conservative and reserved, rarely showing their emotions. She never heard them use angry words with each other and fighting between the girls was forbidden. While Marie felt the rebellion of her teenage peers, she knew her parents would not condone rudeness or sarcasm. To this day, she couldn't conceive of disagreeing with her parents.

Perhaps you can better understand why Dick accepts and occasionally enjoys Stephanie's strong-willed behaviour while Marie barely tolerates it. Stephanie's grandparents, siblings and friends respond differently to her behaviour, depending upon the meaning they give it. Her friends respect her for standing up to her parents. Her aunts and uncles view her behaviour with relief knowing they are not the only parents with obnoxious teenagers. Her younger siblings see her as a leader, breaking new ground so their way will be easier.

Your anger is determined by your values. It is not caused by external events or people. You, *and you alone*, are responsible for your anger. You can control your emotions, if you choose to. You need not be the victim of your emotional responses. You have a free choice about how you want to feel and how you will react to others. Your success in the game of life will depend entirely on those strategic choices. That's the way it is with all of your hot buttons.

EXPRESSING YOUR ANGER

The key to anger management lies in your ability to do a *cost-benefit analysis*—weighing the costs of getting angry with the benefits that can be gained by not getting angry. Or, depending on the way you handle your anger, you might consider the costs of not getting angry with the benefits of displaying your anger. (If you never show your anger, it could be a tactical advantage to get angry once in a while.)

Should you decide there is an advantage to displaying your anger, you need to consider the most appropriate way to do so. Your anger should accomplish something. Controlled anger can be a positive force in the game. Here are a few guidelines to consider when using anger to your advantage:

Make sure you are angry with the right person. Don't blame a subordinate for a mistake that more properly rests with a supervisor. Misplaced anger can undermine relationships you could better use for support. If you do express unjustified anger with a person in front of others, it's only fair that you apologize in front of others.

Keep your remarks focused on the issues, not on the person. Criticize his specific behaviour or performance, not his intelligence or character. "I statements" help you focus on behaviour while alerting the other person to your feelings. It's hard to argue with feelings anyway. "You statements", on the other hand, create defensiveness. Instead of "You always make a mess of these things", try "I feel annoyed when I see the mess that you've made."

Make it clear why you are angry. If her procrastination has forced you to waste your time and is the trigger for your anger, make that fact known. Remember to use "I statements"—"I am angry you didn't get that done when you promised you would."

Don't refer to a person's family, race, religion, social class, appearance or personal habits. This will only create defensiveness and divert their attention from the real issue. These topics are value-laden and will inevitably lead to an escalation of the conflict.

Don't dwell on the past. Refer only to the situation immediately at hand. Holding a grudge keeps you in the past and it stresses you, not her. Relationships are about the present and the future, not the past.

Don't make threats (especially ones you can't keep). You may have second thoughts after you cool off; you will then be forced to back down and your reputation will be at risk. Threats typically lead to counterthreats and further conflict escalation.

Don't limit the other person's anger. When you shout, others instinctively shout back. Mutual anger can clear the air. But if you take the position that you can become angry and the other person cannot, he will rightly resent your arrogance. Now you will have something to fight about.

Whenever possible, give the other person a way out. If a co-worker offers to rectify or apologize for an offense, don't continue the fight. Recognize when you've achieved your objective.

You do have a right to be angry. It is legally permitted. But the critical issue is whether (and how) it will be to your advantage. When you choose to be angry, are you expressing yourself in a way that can improve the situation, make you feel better and gain you respect? Or, as Andrew Bierce once observed, "Speak when you are angry and you will make the best speech you will ever regret."

When you learn to manage the anger button, you will feel greater zest, joy, peace, freedom, productivity and enlightenment. It is a choice you can make. Attitudes can be put on in the morning as deliberately as a suit of clothes. If you decide to put on a cheerful, collaborative outlook in the morning, you will find it exceedingly difficult to get sucked into someone's game later in the day.

ICEBERGS

Beyond managing your hot buttons, you need to be wary of other barriers that prevent you from winning the game. I call them "icebergs" because the dangerous part is what is concealed or what may lie below the surface. The icebergs we must navigate to play the game well include hidden agendas, double standards, assumptions and rumours.

Hidden Agendas. Often the real concerns in an encounter between players are expressed in an inappropriate way or at an inopportune moment. Sometimes these hidden agendas are used knowingly by skilled players as weapons or traps. They invariably appear from a direction you least expect. Uncovering a purposefully hidden agenda is not an easy task. Good listening skills are essential. By listening to the exact words, you can frequently detect inconsistencies in voice tone and body language. These incongruencies often reveal the existence of a hidden agenda.

The best tactic for flushing out a hidden agenda is to be direct. Outline a formal, explicit agenda. Ask: *"What things do we want to talk about?"* Make a list of the topics you both view as relevant to the matter under discussion. Agendas are powerful tools that can serve a multitude of useful purposes in conflict situations. Here is a partial list of the benefits a properly developed agenda delivers:

- Structures the conflict by outlining the issues

- Enables the issues to be prioritized

- Assists in good time management

- Focuses or forces closure

- Enables "win-win" trade-offs

- Keeps the discussion on track

- Provides a record of what was discussed

- Limits the conflict (keeps out irrelevant topics)

- Facilitates preparation (what you need to know)

- Alters expectations (an information-giving device)

Anticipate and plan for hidden agendas. Don't be blind-sided by what lies below the surface. Insist on an explicit agenda and use it as a tool for generating positive conflict.

Double Standards. Perhaps the most treacherous icebergs to navigate around are the seemingly irreconcilable value differences that separate and divide us, especially those we call double standards. When we believe that others should conform to our expectations of performance, even though we may not feel compelled to observe these same standards or restrictions on our own behaviour, we are espousing a double standard. Since we live by our values and our expectations as to what constitutes proper behaviour, it is unlikely we will change these views easily. To deal with the double standard in a conflict situation, focus the discussion on consequences. Operationalize the double standard. Here is an example.

Sam is the chief architect at Pyramid Ltd., a large building design firm in the lower mainland. Several months ago, he hired Laurie, a promising young designer. When he interviewed Laurie, there was no question in Sam's mind that she was the best candidate for the job.

The entire staff of Pyramid has been invited to Ace Construction's open-house cocktail party to celebrate the opening of its latest facility. Because Sam wants to maintain a good relationship with his firm's biggest client, he urges each of his staff members to attend the "schmooze" and to bring a guest. Since he has never heard Laurie mention a male friend, he fully expects to see her alone at the party.

Laurie arrives at the party with a female friend. It quickly becomes obvious to all that they are much more than just friends. Their affection for one another is explicitly, if not blatantly, demonstrated. Observing this display, Mr. Challmers, the conservative vice-president of Ace Construction, pulls Sam aside and advises that he does not approve of "such a couple" being present at a company function, especially with some of their key accounts in attendance. In fact, his wife is "really ticked off." He strongly suggests that Sam take "whatever steps are necessary to remedy this awkward situation *immediately*."

If you were Sam, how would you handle this situation?

You could order Laurie and her guest to leave. But she may resent your coercive approach and decide to make a scene. After all, her sexual preference is a legally-protected right. She knows this and she is also probably incensed by the affront in this particular setting. An argument about one's values and, ultimately, one's rights will rarely produce an amicable resolution. Rather, the conflict is likely to become an emotional one and escalate.

More constructively, you might choose to move the confrontation away from personal values. You need to find an issue that will reduce the emotional intensity a values conflict typically engenders. A discussion of the *appropriateness* of the behaviour (not the rights of the individual) in the context of these specific circumstances would be far less threatening to Laurie. In which case, she would be more receptive to an understanding of the common predicament. Judging or imposing one's standards will only energize the conflict.

Assumptions. It is human nature to make assumptions. But our assumptions, especially when combined with those of the other player, represent more icebergs standing in the way of constructive problem solving. Indeed, we sometimes create a conflict, where none might exist, by assuming the worst possible scenario. Although we like to think we don't make too many assumptions, such is not the case. That awareness alone can enable you to pay closer attention to these icebergs. The following task is instructive and enlightening.

Read the paragraph below once (or at least not more than twice) and then follow the direction given:

A businessman had just turned off the lights in the store when a man appeared and demanded money. The owner opened a cash register. The contents of the cash register were scooped up and the man sped away. A member of the police was notified promptly.

As you read the following sentences, circle **T** if you know the statement is true, **F** is it is false, or **?** of you don't know.

A man appeared after the owner turned off his store lights.	T	F	?
The robber was a man.	T	F	?
The man did not demand money.	T	F	?
The man who opened the cash register was the owner.	T	F	?
The store owner scooped up the cash register contents.	T	F	?
Someone opened up the cash register.	T	F	?
After the man who demanded the money scooped up the contents of the register, he ran away.	T	F	?
While the cash register contained money, the story does not say how much.	T	F	?
The robber demanded money of the owner.	T	F	?
The story concerns a series of events in which only three persons are mentioned.	T	F	?
This is what happened: someone demanded money, a cash register was opened, its contents were scooped up and a man dashed out of the store.	T	F	?

Now total each column to determine how many T's, F's and ?'s you selected.

If you're like most people, you probably chose more than one "T" and one "F". Yet there is only one categorically true statement in the paragraph (someone did open the cash register). Only one false statement (the man did not demand money). The rest of the statements are neither true nor false, based on the information provided. Hence, they require question marks. T and F scores higher than 1 indicate the number of assumptions you made. As you can see, we do make a lot of assumptions. It's quite normal. But imagine how many assumptions you make in a conflict situation, when emotions are aroused and information is difficult to ascertain. To navigate these icebergs, we must be wary of the assumptions we make about the other person, the situation at hand and the issues in dispute.

Rumours. Often the basis of our conflicts with others is information derived through second or even third-hand sources. We rarely are witnesses to the issues or so-called facts in dispute. Someone usually tells us about them. But we tend to use that information as if it were an accurate, first-hand account. The problem, of course, is that such information is rarely accurate and the reasons for its distortion are numerous. The observations or conclusions initially determined were perceived by someone and, therefore, filtered through his value system. None of us actually "sees" reality; rather, we see our own unique version of it. What we take in through our senses is altered by our biases, assumptions and prior experiences. To both understand and communicate it, we give this new experience a label. Rarely, however, will two people use the same labels to describe similar sensory experiences.

Added to this distortion is a phenomenon known as closure. Quickly draw a circle on a piece of paper. The odds are great that, in your haste, the two ends of the circle do not actually connect. There is likely a small space at the top of your circle (assuming you started at the top). So far so good? Now ask someone to describe what you have just drawn.

Research indicates that almost eighty percent of those who view this drawing will immediately describe it as a circle. Some more imaginative types might see an apple, an orange, a ball and so on. In fact, this hastily drawn figure is not a circle, since the lines at the top are not joined together. An incomplete circle perhaps. But, in searching for an appropriate label to describe the illustration, most of us tend to "fill in" the missing piece. This is a natural tendency for most people. We have a desire to bring closure on the information to make it more intelligible. We close the circle to make it conform to our existing knowledge or labels. We do this because we like things neat and tidy. We detest ambiguity. (This is, of course, a cultural bias; some people are quite comfortable with ambiguity.)

When we receive information, especially emotionally-charged gossip, we have a tendency to do two things: add in information and eliminate "the fuzzies" to achieve neatness. The result is inaccurate data and on this we base our judgments (or is it our assumptions?).

Our ability to interpret information is predicated on good listening and observation skills. None of us is sufficiently skilled to ensure 100 percent accuracy. Rumour clinics are teaching exercises designed to demonstrate the inadequacy of second-hand information. Members of a group are asked to leave the room while the remainder study a one-paragraph description of a typical situation involving colleagues in the workplace. When one person in the group is satisfied that he has mastered the information well enough to accurately describe the details, one of the departing members is invited back into the room to hear the story. (The rest you can no doubt surmise.) With each retelling, the story becomes more distorted, often to bizarre proportions. Information is added and deleted. Values, stereotypes and assumptions become apparent. Yet the curious thing is that the participants are genuinely trying to be accurate in their retelling of the story. They are aware that their colleagues are charting their every embellishment or deletion. In real life, we are not placed in such a fish bowl of scrutiny. But the result is similar.

In your own life, how many conflicts are caused by inaccurate, second-hand information? To avoid these icebergs, you must acknowledge that neither party has all the information needed to resolve the issue at hand. What information you do have is, in all likelihood, not accurate. Listen to the exact words. Ask questions. Probe for logical pieces that may be missing. The passage of time will diminish your ability to recall information accurately. Indeed, most people forget 80% of what they hear within 48 hours of hearing it.

Now that you understand the purpose of the game and some of the obstacles to playing it effectively, let's move on to the rules. This further knowledge is vital to your success in dealing with the more skilled and challenging players.

✧ THE RULES

Every game has rules. Your understanding of these rules will determine your degree of success in the game. The more you learn and practise them, the more often you win.

In the proper sense of the word, there are no universally accepted "rules" governing interpersonal transactions. We may agree that certain principles and norms, when practised, give rise to "civilized" behaviour. But a code of conduct is a very personal thing, depending on one's values. For the purpose of playing the game of life, however, the following principles constitute the *ground rules for success*:

1. *Life is a game of power, real and imagined.* Your success depends on your ability to understand and manage the distribution of power between (or among) the players. Knowing how to reduce or remove power as the sole determinant in the game is critical to achieving your objectives. Otherwise, despite the consequences, whomever has it will win. It's that simple. Whether you are the top dog or the underdog, you need to know what power is, how to use it and how to counter it.

2. *Your greatest asset is your own creative genius.* In the game of life, your objective is to find a way to outsmart, rather than out-muscle, your adversary. An inventive player is a winning player. If you take the time to think creatively, there's always a better approach or a more effective tactic to dealing with obstacles. And there's usually a more creative way to express it. Because what counts in the game is not what you say, but how you choose to say it.

3. *Empathic listening is the competitive advantage.* Information is the ultimate source of power in the game of life. Those who have it control the game. That's because it's what you *don't* know that can hurt you. Beyond the value of knowing, listening is the quickest way to build trust between opposing players and trust is the essence of rapport and the ability to influence others.

4. *Recognize who you're playing.* If you don't know who you're playing, you can't know what game you're playing. And, if you don't know the game, you can't

win. A knowledge of your opponent's behavioural traits, needs and weaknesses enables the necessary emotional distance to make smarter tactical choices. An aware player cannot be a victim.

5. *Confront the opposing behaviour* (sensitively and intelligently). You must hold others accountable for their actions whenever their behaviour is contrary to your objectives. Artful confrontation will minimize the potential for escalation and make others responsible for solution finding. You can't play the game well if either player is out of control. When you can control yourself, you can take charge of the game.

6. *Goals are achieved through influence, not force*. Influence is a trial and error process with methods as varied as the people involved. This requires a process orientation to the game and the realization that quick is synonymous with risk. We have to overcome the barriers that prevent us from seeing how and why we react to others in the way we do. When we understand this key principle, with the right tactics, we can invariably influence the desired outcomes.

7. *Preparation is the name of the game*. There is an inverse relationship between the amount of time spent preparing for the contest and the speed at which you can reach your desired destination. Preparation enables you to ask the right questions (and, of course, know which questions are the right ones). Adequate preparation is the most important stage of the game.

Heeding these seven ground rules for success will make you a better player. These principles are the foundation for every move and every choice you make. Each one is described in detail in the following chapters. As you come to appreciate their importance and function in the game, and as you refine them through practice to fit your own unique playing style, the game will become simpler, less stressful and more enjoyable. And winning will become much more probable.

3 POWER

Power is perceived.

Few words in the English language can evoke the emotional response of the word *power*. Although I see the game board defined as conflict, some might argue that the board on which the game of life is played is really one of power. An awareness of the nature and dynamics of power is therefore central to understanding how interpersonal and business relationships function. Your knowledge of the concept of power is critical to your success in the game. This is ground rule number one.

Having power in a relationship is largely a matter of possessing control. Power is the ability to either control yourself or to control the other person. Preferably, it is both. Once you possess the requisite skills to manage power in relationships, you will be in a position to get things done. Which is the purpose of exercising power—to get things done according to your needs, goals and aspirations.

Power is often misunderstood. Some believe power to be finite. This implies that there's "only so much of it to go around." Like a pie with six slices, if I take four for myself then only two remain for you. The assumption is false. The pie can be sliced into many pieces. The pie can also be made bigger. Power has an almost infinite number of sources and is infinite in its uses.

Another myth about power is the self-defeating premise that the other players have more of it than do you. A further assumption, given such a premise, is that you can't increase what you don't have. On analysis, both notions are incorrect.

THE POWER EQUATION

In every relationship, there exists an imbalance of power. Power is neither equally distributed between the parties nor is it static. Depending on the people and the situation, it is constantly shifting and fluid. This dynamic "disequilibrium" is perhaps best explained by viewing power as an equation. Your ability to understand this equation and manage it will greatly influence your chances of success in the game.

Think for a moment of a marriage, either of a business or marital kind. In a marriage, we assume power to be equally distributed between the parties. But it isn't. In a healthy marriage, power constantly shifts from partner to partner depending on the circumstances. On some occasions, one person clearly has more power than the other. In other situations, the reverse is true. Out of this dynamic disequilibrium grows love, honour and respect for the strengths and talents of the other partner.

Let's examine an unhealthy relationship. Frank and Pearl, married for 27 years, appear content with their many accomplishments. The problem is that their power equation is permanently imbalanced. It's stuck in a one-sided tilt. Let's go back to the beginning.

Before deciding to spend the rest of their lives together, Frank and Pearl sat down to discuss their life's goals and roles. They discovered they shared common aspirations, among them a family (they desired a girl and a boy, both of whom would be university educated) and a house with a white picket fence. Their values could be defined as conservative and mid-American. Having found compatibility in what they wanted to accomplish together, they then discussed their roles: who would do what to ensure the achievement of their mutual aspirations. Again, they were of like mind.

It was agreed that Frank, a blue-collar worker, would be the breadwinner. He would also take responsibility for the family budget. And a frugal one it would be. Pearl agreed to stay at home, providing dutiful domestic support in pursuit of their goals. She would not only bake the bread (literally), she would make her own clothes, as well as the children's, as her contribution to making ends meet.

The years pass. For the most part, Frank and Pearl realize their shared aspirations: two kids, the house paid for in the 17th year, and so on. But something is not right in this relationship. With the children now gone and a sizeable nest egg accumulating in the bank (the result of years of ultra-conservative investing), Pearl is beginning to question her role. Like many her age, she's experiencing the anxiety that precipitates personal growth.

Pearl increasingly feels they should be enjoying some of their liquid investments because "you can't take it with you." After scrimping throughout her married years, she would at least like to buy a new wardrobe. She feels she's entitled to it. Since they can now afford it, why not a second honeymoon as well? Two weeks in Hawaii, perhaps, to revisit the topic of their goals and roles. And their future together.

Frank stands opposed to "this nonsense". After all, they didn't get where they are today by spending hard earned dollars frivolously. Naturally, he loves Pearl's clothes "just the way they are." His budgetary system has not just succeeded, it has become an obsession. (Frank is not entirely obtuse, however. He's not opposed to Pearl's vacation idea. It's just that his view of "getting away" is a February weekend in Buffalo, on the family plan, when the rates are more affordable. After all, isn't that how they managed to get where they are today?)

Who has the power in this relationship? Clearly, Frank does. Their power equation is tilted in one direction. Indeed, it's static. Pearl is entirely dependent upon Frank's control—to which they both initially agreed—of the family purse strings. So Frank has the power and Pearl doesn't.

The more important question is: what can Pearl do about the situation? She could sit down and have a talk with Frank and attempt to reason with him. She could endeavour to renegotiate their original understanding. However, given Frank's inordinate power position, that would be fruitless. Some things in life are rather simple. One of them is that *when you have the power, you really don't have to negotiate with people.* (Because, when everyone has spoken, the result invariably is "my way or the highway.")

Although Pearl could take more drastic measures to curtail or even undermine Frank's power, her purpose is not to threaten him. Besides, when you come to understand the power equation, you begin to discover that your power can be increased without diminishing that of the other player. Sure, taking power away from others might be easy. But power can be enhanced independently. That's what intelligent and artful players do in seeking win-win outcomes.

What can Pearl do to alter this power imbalance? For starters, she could get a job. I say "for starters" because the first step in power enhancement is the most difficult. But, once you've initiated the process of self-empowerment, the rest is easier. It's like throwing a pebble into a pond; it has a ripple effect.

In Pearl's case, the simple act of getting a part-time job can increase her power and thereby alter the power equation with Frank. With her new employment status comes a pay cheque that belongs to her, not Frank. She now has the independent means to buy something for herself, perhaps a new dress or shoes. As a result, she begins to feel better about herself. Therein lies the power of self-esteem and confidence.

And the ripple effect? Feeling better about herself, Pearl begins to widen her social network. She feels confident in meeting others. She is developing a new power base of friends. This is known as the power of affiliation. And the momentum continues...eventually to the point where she feels sufficiently self-assured to discuss with Frank "their future together." She exudes a newly found confidence and this results in a more constructive, both-win negotiation.

When the power equation is in balance, when power becomes less of a determinant in the outcome of the game, discussions are more creative and fruitful, and agreements are more stable and long lasting. When the equation is unbalanced and static, losers feel their loss is attributable solely to their power disadvantage, not to the merits of their argument.

An understanding of the power equation should lead you to reflect on the role power plays in relationships. It might also lead you to contemplate the notion of "giving up power" when you have too much of it and your objective is to achieve a win-win solution. Since it is difficult to actually reduce your power, you endeavour to either share your power or create the perception that you have less power than you actually do. This is a winning strategy when dealing with subordinates or with children, people who have less power than you.

How do you do it? If you understand the power equation and the objective of reducing your power to achieve both-win outcomes, you're well on your way. Creative tactics usually follow when the problem has been adequately defined. In dealing with children who have misbehaved, for example, take the time to observe what happens when you replace the parental "judge, jury, and executioner" role with that of a "partner in crime" relationship. After all, wasn't there a time in your youth when you too may have misbehaved in a similar fashion? In your child's eyes, at the moment you reduce your power, the equation comes into balance. The result is more likely an open and honest effort to resolve a problem, rather than an attempt to resist your power and, in the process, resent you further.

PRINCIPLES OF POWER

As you've seen, power is relative. Rarely does one side enjoy complete power. It is shared and the distribution can be artfully managed. The more you understand the concept of the power equation, the better equipped you will be to play the game. It will come as no surprise that winning is easier when you have a power advantage. So here are some further principles of power for your reflection:

- *Power is perceived.* We all have more power than we think we have. If you think you've got it, then you've got it. If you think you don't have it (even when you do), then you don't have it.

- *Power can be exerted without action.* If the other player expects that some action might or will be taken against him, he will react in some fashion.

- *Power is always limited.* Its scope and range depend entirely upon the player, her understanding of power dynamics, the situation, prevailing regulations, ethical standards, the desired present or future relationship, and more.

- *Power exists when it is accepted.* Some people are less willing to be dominated by powerful people than are others. They would rather do without than submit to exploitation. They challenge and resist the presumption of authority.

- *The ends of power cannot be separated from the means.* One cannot hope or expect to convince others solely through the use of coercive or exploitive tactics.

- *The exercise of power entails cost and risk.* Which is why you have to know how and when to exercise power in the game.

- *Power relationships change over time.* Power changes relationships and power in relationships is fluid and dynamic (hence the concept of an equation constantly in flux).

Power can take many forms. It is not restricted to possessing what someone else doesn't have or what someone else wants. The sources of power (and thus the ability to increase your power advantage in the game) are virtually limitless. Among the many forms of power are these:

- *The power of competition.* You have what someone else wants (and therein lies your power over him).

- *The power of legitimacy.* The ability to use policies, tradition, the way things "ought to be" and the printed word to gain advantage.

- *The power of risk taking.* The willingness and attendant comfort of knowing you can and will take calculated risks.

- *The power of timing.* A knowledge of process, deadlines and the pressures associated with their use and management.

- *The power of hard work.* From doing the homework necessary to adequately prepare for the encounter to simply "out hustling" the other players.

- *The power of a supportive team.* This can serve to lessen the stress or increase the options and alternatives available.

- *The power of skill, expertise and experience.* Derived from playing the game as a conscientious learner.

- *The power of knowing* (or knowing how to discover) your adversary's needs.

- *The power of creativity.* The subject of the following chapter.

Skilful players come to appreciate the importance of power in playing the game. They come to realize it is unlimited in its creation and application. And they discover how to manage its use to their competitive advantage.

4 CREATIVITY

Inventive players are winning players.

Creativity is essential to playing the game of life. Creative players have the ability to escape existing perceptual and behavioural barriers to open up new ways of seeing constructive alternatives and win-win outcomes. Regardless of who may appear to have the power in the contest, successful players know the key to winning consistently lies in out-thinking and outsmarting the other player.

Unfortunately, most people underestimate their creative potential. They are unaware or unconvinced that, within each of us, lies a creative genius waiting to be unleashed. The reason for this self-limiting perception is largely one of socialization; we have learned to be "uncreative" when confronted by troubling circumstances or, worse, people who oppose our views and aspirations. Educator Neil Postman once observed that, as naturally inquisitive children, we "enter schools as question marks only to leave as periods."

The barriers to creativity go beyond those imposed by formal education, time, money, policy, tradition, experience, assumptions, habits, and more. The way a problem is defined, the amount of information we have (either too much or too little), our environment and our motivation can all block our ability to conceive ideas and find innovative solutions. For some, the list of barriers that limit creative potential seems virtually endless.

Yet, on analysis, these barriers are largely a matter of perception. We create our "boxes" and sustain and reinforce these comfort zones in our mind. They become convenient excuses for inaction, rationalizations that enable us to align our actual performance with our expectations of performance. These barriers to creative thought also become ammunition in the hands of those who oppose our ideas and our objectives.

Consider the barrier of fear—of failure, rejection or ridicule. It is our fear of the encounters and the consequences of dealing with challenging people and difficult situations that often makes us incapable of effective action and appropriate counter-tactics. Without effective or novel strategies for influencing these players, we invariably reinforce their difficult behaviour and make the situation worse. But, since fear is largely a function of where we choose to focus our attention, it is a self-imposed limitation, or a barrier that need not be.

FOCUS ON THE SOLUTION

In understanding how fear can undermine our ability to play the game creatively, we need only consider this illustration. What if, for example, I place a long piece of wood on the floor and ask you to "walk the plank." As an incentive, I offer you one dollar if you're successful in walking from one end to the other without falling off. First, you consider the dimensions of the board: 12 inches wide, 6 inches thick and 30 feet long. No problem, you say. And you're right! You walk the plank and quickly collect your dollar.

Now we alter the circumstances. Instead of putting the plank on the floor, we place it at the top of two 10-story buildings about 30 feet apart. Just as the risks have increased, so too have the rewards. Should you successfully walk the plank at this altitude, I will give you $100,000. Would you accept the offer?

Probably not. So what's changed? Although the task remains the same, the consequences of failure (if you think about them, that is) have become far greater. Your enthusiasm for the challenge wanes proportionately. The fear (of failure) you now experience is entirely a function of where you have chosen to focus your attention. Were you to focus on the task at hand (which you've already proven is a relatively simple task), rather than on the ground below and the consequences of failure, you would succeed quite easily.

Creative people don't focus their attention on failing. They focus squarely on succeeding. They recognize that their barriers, especially those they might have to confront in dealing with difficult encounters, are perceived rather than real. They don't use brute force to overcome these self-imposed limitations. Instead, they tend to ask a series of artful, probing and intelligent questions designed to reveal alternatives, options and opportunities. They transcend the barriers to winning with creativity.

Those who choose to focus on why they cannot be successful in influencing others are linear thinkers. They see only what prevents them from accomplishing their goal, not what will enable them to achieve it. Linear thinkers do the obvious; they take the safe, tried and true course of action. They do what is expected of them and therein lies the reason for their lack of success in dealing with more skilled players. They are reasonable people who seek to employ rational methods of persuasion in influencing the behaviour of their adversaries. These methods are rarely successful, especially with challenging people who have refined their game over a lifetime and who are now immune to our reasonable tactics.

Lateral thinkers go in the not-so-obvious direction. They take the path less travelled. They use their intuition and, often as not, they do what they're *not* expected to do. In dealing with troublesome people, this is usually the better strategy. Because the people we find the most difficult are the ones who have prepared for the obvious.

They have developed skilful defences against rational methods of persuasion and are thus prepared to counter expected tactics of communication.

To be creative in playing the game is to broaden your perceptual horizon. Think of differing viewpoints as "windows" on reality. *Different windows provide different perspectives.* Our windows determine how much or how little of the "real world" we actually see. Window, in this example, is a metaphor for our value system. The pane is the filter through which we judge what we see. Our windows define our personalities and our unique point of view. Their windows, of course, likewise define a different point of view. The ability to "take in" the sum of these perspectives, to broaden our perceptual horizon, can make us better players.

CREATIVE PROBLEM SOLVING

The object in dealing with opposing players is not to argue the rightness of your point of view but to find a viewing point that helps you understand theirs. From this vantage point, you can creatively develop a strategy to influence their behaviour. Once you reach this objective height, you can scan the horizon for artful, tactful and thus more appropriate responses.

The concept of windows is a creative thinking tool—one that enables you to rise above the encounter to become tactically aware and astute. Your attention is not focused solely on defensive or offensive manoeuvres but on a range of creative options. The question now is which of these tactical alternatives is the best response given the nature of your adversary, his strategy, viewpoint and the situation at hand.

Every creative problem-solving process starts at the same place. You begin by trying to gain a thorough understanding of the problem. In confronting another player, you must ask yourself *"what's the problem here?"* Uncreative people look for the solution before they truly understand the nature of the problem. A problem well defined is half solved.

Albert Einstein perhaps said it best. He was once confronted by a journalist who asked the following question: "If you had but one hour to solve the greatest problem facing mankind today, how would you spend that time?" After reflecting on the question, Einstein replied, "I would take 55 minutes to truly understand the nature of the problem and I am convinced that the right answer would come to me in the last 5 minutes."

How many of us tackle our people challenges or develop our game strategies in that same deliberate manner? Thomas Edison put another spin on creative problem solving when he said it was comprised of 99% perspiration and 1% inspiration. More work in thinking through the challenge leads to better results.

Once you've defined the problem, you must clearly establish your objectives.

A headlong rush to solutions will lead you to contemplate little more than the obvious. To be effective, you want an innovative approach to dealing with the other player's tactics. Begin by thinking about what it is you really want to accomplish, remembering that good objectives must be specific, measurable, realistic and achievable.

It's pointless to say, "I want Harry to stop being such a jerk!" There is no specificity in this objective. You're also engaging in character assassination (even though Harry may be acting like a jerk, isn't he really just looking through a different window than are you?). A more measurable and realistic goal is to say something like this: "I wish Harry would listen to my point of view before he gives me his." Whether this objective is achievable is now a function of your ability to utilize the right tactics.

Once the objective is known, the focus of your attention should be on what's preventing you from achieving it. We're not interested in solutions yet. We need to know the barriers to success. Let's not think about how to get Harry to listen. That would be too rational. Rather, focus your attention on what's *preventing* Harry from listening to you. Focus for the moment on the obstacles to your objectives, not on how you can achieve them.

Now you can move on to the search for appropriate tactical responses. Consider how you might remove those things that impair Harry's ability or willingness to listen to your viewpoint. Be creative. Use your imagination. The results will amaze you (as well as Harry).

Outsmarting the players you encounter in the game is a discipline that can be learned, provided you are willing to practise until you've aquired it.

REPROGRAM YOUR SOFTWARE

When it comes to unleashing our creativity, each of us is blessed with the same hardware: our brain. It is the source of our creative genius. What distinguishes us from others in our ability to solve people puzzles and play the game well is not our hardware. To achieve success in our interpersonal relations, we need to reprogram our software. As we age, this software can become outmoded. Our tactical responses become habitual and unthinking. We fit old solutions into new problems. Our reactions to changing challenges become predictable and ineffective.

There are certain "afflictions" that can seriously impair our software and thus our creative potential as we advance in years. By early adulthood, some people begin suffering from "analexia." This is a predisposition to analyse virtually everything in life, to quantify rather than to qualify the important things. Those who are analexic talk about "the bottom line" or say "that just doesn't add up." They compare their achievements to others. Salaries become scorecards. If it can't be measured, it doesn't exist.

If an antidote to this software virus is not discovered, the ability to consider artful and inventive solutions to life's many challenges is severely diminished. If the affliction worsens, it leads one into a debilitating state called "psychosclerosis," which is literally a "hardening of the categories." Our thinking software now functions by compartmentalizing experience, fitting life into fixed, rigid boxes. If our sensory data fit into those boxes, it is accepted. If it doesn't, it is rejected. The result is stereotypical thinking—seeing what we expect to see, not what is really happening. We see life passing us by through one, very small window.

Should our software degenerate further, we risk succumbing to a software virus that can cripple our interpersonal effectiveness. It's called "analoculosis." Simply put, this is a miserable state of mind which is analogous to fusing the sphincter muscle with the optic nerve. The result is a crappy outlook on just about everything.

However facetious these software defects might appear, they provide important food for thought. Because, in the game of life, you have choices to make. You can choose to unleash your creative genius in dealing with other players. You can choose artful and intelligent tactical responses. You can choose to be unfettered by narrow vision (psychosclerosis). You can choose to transcend your barriers by focusing on success rather than on what prevents you from winning. Or you can choose to be manipulated, bullied, frustrated or confused. That choice is entirely yours.

It takes a creative thinker to win consistently. Creative players know that the barriers to success are largely mind-sets. They know the insight that leads to the right game strategy is rarely the initial reaction. When confronted by a challenging player, they take the time to examine the problem from another vantage point. That's rarely obvious. But it is creative.

5 LISTENING

Listen in their language, not yours.

We spend almost 80 percent of our waking hours communicating with one another. About 30 percent of this time is spent talking to others, 16 percent writing, 9 percent reading and 45 percent listening. Although we were taught how to read, write and speak, who taught us how to listen?

Let's start with the premise that we are all lousy listeners. We have two eyes, two ears and one mouth. Those who play the game well use these communication vehicles in exactly those proportions. While we may hear the words that are spoken, we seldom listen to what they actually mean. And few of us listen to understand what the words mean to the speaker.

Listening is a powerful influencing skill. Yet many things impair our ability to be good listeners. Hearing is a natural act: soundwaves enter the auditory canal and vibrate against the ear drum. Listening, on the other hand, occurs only when you have the discipline, energy and commitment to focus your attention on what is being said and what it actually means (both to you and the speaker). Hardly natural and certainly not easy.

Despite the challenge, listening can generate extraordinary benefits in the game of life. Not only do you ascertain the information needed to respond in tactical and tactful ways, you also communicate an invaluable message. Listening makes a statement. It says, *"I'm interested in what you have to say and, therefore, I'm interested in you as a person."* Listening is the simplest trust-building tactic in the game. When people trust you, they give you quality information—they tell you what you need to know to be a better player. If your tactics are predicated on the quality of information you receive during your encounters, consider the distinct advantage a good listener has in making the right strategic choices. As winning players know, quality information is the ultimate source of power.

In conflict situations, where emotional intensity runs high, listening also serves as a great leveller. When we shout back at others, their rage is legitimized and energized. It is impossible to sustain your anger in the presence of an empathic listener—one who acknowledges your feelings as much as your words.

BARRIERS TO LISTENING

Why are we such poor listeners? It isn't necessarily that we rarely have the

47

time, interest or inclination to listen. Many things constitute barriers to effective listening and most of them occur naturally in our daily lives. That's why it takes such enormous concentration and willpower to overcome them.

Your psychological state at any given moment can make you a selective listener. Known as "wishful hearing", it determines what information you take in and what importance you personally attach to it. This unique perspective on the world is a function of your individual personality. A euphoric, optimistic person and a depressed, downcast individual will take entirely different meanings from the same message. It's as simple as that and there's little you can do to correct it. If you could, would you change your temperament just to improve your listening ability? Not likely.

Then there's our attention span. Research suggests the average adult has a focused attention span of about seven seconds. Incredible, but apparently true. Our short attention span—that time when we focus completely on what is being said—is largely the result of the differentials in our talking speed (which is variously estimated to be about 100-300 words per minute), our listening speed (400-800 w.p.m) and our thinking speed (1200-1500 w.p.m., because we also think in images). In other words, we are more proficient listeners than we are talkers and, since "a picture can be worth 1,000 words", faster thinkers than listeners. Listening to a slow, boring speaker (without extreme concentration) is an opportunity to think of other things. Not surprisingly, this is what we usually do.

The list of barriers to effective listening is virtually endless: different conversation styles, language accents and idioms, the relevance of the topic, visual and noise distractions, environmental factors, our biases, the tendency to stereotype people and situations, and our feelings about the speaker, to name a few.

Indeed, *how good a listener are you?* On a scale of 100, where would you likely rate your listening efficiency? Take a moment to think about it. Research indicates that the vast majority of people possess a listening efficiency rate in the fifteen to twenty-five percent range. Did you assume your listening rate was higher? Perhaps it is. Those whom we deem to be "phenomenal" listeners, of which there are precious few, measure in at about the sixty percent level. Which means that they too miss a lot of vital information. And these tests were not conducted during conflict situations where emotional stress is so high that distortion of meaning is inevitable.

GETTING BETTER

The listening challenge confronts every player in the game. The good news is that listening is a skill that can be learned and, with continuing practice, improved dramatically. The essential ingredients for becoming a better listener and, in the process, adding a potent weapon to your arsenal of game skills are these:

- *Be conscious of good listening requirements.* Begin the act of listening by attempting to vacuum your mind of any preconceived notions, preferences or personal aversions toward the speaker. Good listeners are non-judgmental listeners. They listen within the talker's frame of reference, trying to determine why he is saying what he says and why he is saying it in the way he has chosen to say it. The objective is to get beyond the words—to listen to the shape of the speaker's innermost thoughts and needs so that the empathy is real. Relating in this way encourages the speaker to reveal candid thoughts.

- *Listen to ascertain both meaning and feelings.* Often the real meaning lies not in what people say but in how they express themselves. Try to be conscious of both the content and the manner in which a viewpoint is expressed. Listen for the thematic chord and do not get sidetracked by incidental remarks or tangential comments.

- *Listening is an act of patience.* Resist the urge to interrupt, contradict or argue. Hold your tongue and hear the other person out. Your patience will always be rewarded. Concentrate on what is being said even though it may seem dull, boring and repetitive. Remember that listening is not easy—because you can listen faster than the other person can talk.

- *Listen with more than your ears.* Listen with your whole body. Make eye contact. Lean forward. Nod occasionally. Avoid body language that suggests disinterest or disagreement—like folding your arms across your chest or leaning away from the speaker. Don't listen like a mute; make a sound from time to time (like "uh-huh") and give positive feedback. Let her know you're actually listening to her words. Learn to "listen" to facial expressions, hand gestures, eyes and body posture, all of which are communicating to you as well.

- *Listen to what is not said.* Like our icebergs, often the real message is contained in what is not heard, in what is omitted, intentionally or not. Beware of attempts to deceive. Note but do not react to attempts to manipulate, flatter, antagonize or shock you. Don't prejudge the speaker or his message because of dress, manners, accent, vocabulary or other personal idiosyncrasies.

- *If you must disagree, never argue.* Arguing only creates defensiveness, resistance and entrenchment. Rather, restate what you heard to the satisfaction of the other person. This reflection ensures quality communication and makes the speaker more receptive to your point of view. Good listeners learn to distinguish fact from opinion, evaluate inferences and detect prejudices and assumptions—all of which is critical to creating understanding between seemingly adversarial viewpoints.

In focusing your attention on the act of listening, be mindful of the impediments to your listening effectiveness. While these are normal human tendencies, they are nonetheless barriers that impair your ability to derive quality information from the other players. The barriers we must overcome include the following:

- the difficulty of clearing the mind of other pressing thoughts, issues and concerns;

- the tendency to speak before we "think through" our remarks and their probable impact on the other person;

- the preference to interrupt rather than reflect on what is being said;

- the desire to dispute those viewpoints with which we disagree;

- the propensity to discard information we don't like or perceive as irrelevant, misinformed or uninteresting;

- the aversion to listening to information that is too complex, detailed or technical;

- the reaction we often have to dismiss statements from people we dislike or consider unimportant;

- the tendency to focus on what we want to say before hearing what the other person is trying to say; and

- the need to jump to conclusions before all the evidence is in.

REFLECTION

Once you've listened, particularly if the words spoken are critical to your position or argument, it's important that you let him know you've heard what he is trying to tell you. This feedback process is called reflection. It's stating in your own words what the other person's comment means to you. The primary goal is to get verification that you have understood the speaker's meaning as it was intended. If you have not understood, reflecting will usually result in the necessary clarification. When either occurs (verification or clarification), you are communicating effectively. This is the first, necessary condition for successfully influencing others.

For example, when you tell somebody your phone number, he will usually repeat it to make sure that he heard correctly (assuming he wants to remember it). However, when you make a complicated statement, most people typically express agreement or disagreement without trying to ensure an understanding of what you intended. Most of us assume we understand what the other person has said. Rarely do we check to confirm the intended meaning.

But how do you know that the remark means the same to you as it does to the speaker? Of course, you could get him to clarify his remark by asking, *"What exactly do you mean?"* or *"Tell me more,"* or simply by saying, *"I don't understand."* After an elaboration, you may still face the same question: "Do I really understand what he's trying to say?" Even though you may feel certain that you understand the intended message, the fact is you are assuming that you do.

If, on the other hand, you were to state in your own words what the remark meant to you, the other person could determine whether or not his message is "coming through" as intended. Then, if he thinks you have misunderstood, he can speak directly to the specific misunderstanding you have revealed.

An additional benefit of reflection is that it tells the other person you are genuinely interested in him. At least, that's how your reflective statement or question is perceived. It indicates that you do want to understand what he is trying to say. It is also entirely self-serving: *by understanding his viewpoint, he will be more willing to listen to yours.* It can, as well, serve to defuse anger, hostility and aggression. When people hear that you've heard them, or are trying to do so, they become less intense. In a word, they relax.

Reflection is a crucial skill in airing conflict. It increases the accuracy of communication and thus the degree of mutual or shared understanding. It conveys your interest in the other person and your effort to understand how he or she views the issues at hand.

Since it is a skill, reflection requires practice to perfect. It is more than simply rephrasing the other person's ideas (or trying to say the same thing with different words.) Such "word swapping" may only result in the illusion of mutual understanding, as in the following example:

Mary: "You know, Jane should never have become a teacher."
Jim: "You mean teaching isn't the right job for her?"
Mary: "Exactly! Teaching is *not* the right job for Jane."

Instead of trying to reword Mary's statement, Jim might have asked himself, "What is she trying to tell me about Jane?" In that case, the conversation might have sounded like this:

Mary: "Jane should never have become a teacher."
Jim: "You mean she is too harsh on children? She expects far more than they can reasonably give?"

Mary: "Oh, no. I meant she has such expensive tastes that she can't ever earn enough as a teacher."

Jim: "Oh, I see. You think she should have chosen a profession that would have ensured her a higher standard of living?"

Mary: "Exactly! Teaching is just not the right job for Jane."

Reflection is not a verbal gimmick. More than an essential communication skill, it's an attitude, a desire to know exactly what the other person is endeavouring to tell you. The next time someone is angry with you or criticizing you, reflect her comments until you have clearly demonstrated that you understand what she is trying to say. Then observe the reaction. Note the effect of good reflection on your understanding of the conflict. Studying the impact of your reflective statements on the other player will help you perfect this important skill.

DESCRIBING FEELINGS

Understanding the feelings of others is not easy. The expression of emotions takes many different forms—in body language, in actions and in words. And any specific expression of feelings may result from a variety of emotions. A blush, for example, might indicate you are pleased; it may also indicate that you feel annoyed, embarrassed or uneasy. Likewise, specific feelings are rarely expressed in the same way. The communication of emotions is often inaccurate and misleading. What looks like an expression of anger may result from hurt feelings, frustration or fear.

Another obstacle to the accurate communication of feelings is that your perception of what another might be feeling is based on different kinds of information. When someone speaks, you observe more than just the words; you note their gestures, voice tone, posture and facial expression. In effect, "all of us" is communicating. In addition, you are aware of the immediate context. For example, you are aware if others are watching your confrontation. You make assumptions about how the situation might be influencing what the other is feeling. And you have your own expectations of what the other's behaviour might mean, based on past experience.

You naturally make inferences from all of this information and these assumptions are further influenced by your emotions. What you perceive the other person to be feeling depends more upon what you are feeling than upon their actions or words. If you are feeling guilty about something, for example, you will likely perceive others as being angry with you.

Despite these challenges, if you want others to respond positively to you, you must help them understand exactly how you feel. The best way to describe a feeling is to name it: *"I feel angry"*; *"I'm embarrassed"*; or *"I feel comfortable with you."* Likewise, if you are genuinely concerned about the other person and your relationship, you must seek to understand his emotional reactions.

We usually describe our ideas more accurately than our feelings. These we express in many different ways while rarely identifying the feeling itself. Since we don't have enough labels to encompass the broad range of our emotions, we invent other ways to describe our feelings. We use similes and metaphors. Someone whose friendly overture had just been rebuffed might say, "*I feel like I just walked into a brick wall.*" Some express their feelings by describing the action they might want to take: "*I'd like to shake you,*" or "*I wish I could just leave.*"

The purpose of accurately describing your feelings is to facilitate the airing of conflict. It gets the key concerns out in the open or "on the table" where you can deal with them constructively. People need to know how you feel if open, honest dialogue is to follow. Negative feelings are signals that something deeper may be at issue or unresolved. To ignore these negative feelings is like ignoring a warning light. Describing your feelings, your inner state, is a vital component of effective conflict communication—one that enables you to understand the real issues on the road to improving relationships and satisfying personal needs, goals and aspirations.

DESCRIBING BEHAVIOUR

If you were discussing a problem about what was happening in your relationship, you would want to discuss what each person does that affects the other. And it wouldn't be easy. Most of us have difficulty describing another's negative behaviour in such a way that he would understand which actions we find annoying or offensive. Instead of describing the offending behaviour, we tend to talk about attitudes, motivations or personality characteristics.

Suppose you were to tell Susan that she is rude (a trait) or that she doesn't care about you or your opinion. Would she understand what you were trying to communicate? Are you closer to a shared understanding? On the other hand, if you were to point out to Susan that several times during the past few minutes she interrupted before you could finish what you were trying to say, she would have a much clearer picture of what was bothering you.

Behaviour description is reporting the specific, observable action of others without placing a value on it as either right or wrong, bad or good, or making accusations or generalizations about the other's motives, attitudes or character. It is telling people what behaviour you are confronting by describing it clearly and specifically. You are describing the visible evidence that is open to anybody's observation. It is helpful to begin with "*I see that...*" or "*I noticed that...*" or "*I heard you say...*" This will remind you that you are trying to describe specific behaviours.

Rather than say, "Jim, you're just rude!" (which borders on character assassination), try "Jim, several times you've cut others off before they had a chance to finish." Rather than "Louise, you're trying to show Harry up" (which is accusatory), say "Louise, you've taken the opposite position on nearly everything Harry suggested."

To develop this skill, you must force yourself to pay attention to specific behaviours and avoid making assumptions. For example, the statement "Sam, you deliberately didn't let me finish", implies that Sam knowingly and intentionally interrupted you. Was it really deliberate? All that is observable is that he cut in before you had finished.

As you practise this useful skill, you will discover that many of your conclusions about others are based less on observable evidence than on your own feelings of insecurity, irritation, jealousy or fear. Accusations that attribute undesirable motives to others are usually expressions of negative feelings toward them rather than accurate or reliable descriptions of their behaviour.

NONJUDGMENTAL LISTENING

This too is a useful listening tactic when your objective is to either ascertain as much information as possible (as in negotiating) or encourage the speaker to become a better problem solver. It is also effective whenever you sense the talker is troubled, about to "blow his stack" or simply needs to get something off his chest. The goal is to neither agree nor disagree with the speaker's thoughts until they have been exhausted. The steps are as follows:

- *Take the time to listen.* Patience is the primary qualification to become a good listener. Even though at times it may seem to be a waste of time, it seldom is. Remember your objectives. If, by listening, you can get the information you require, shorten the queue of people with problems at your door or help people to unload their emotional baggage, it's well worth the investment of time.

- *Be attentive.* Give the impression you are genuinely interested in what is being said. Be an empathic listener. If the speaker launches into a tirade, let it flow without interruption until it has been fully vented. It may be mentally trying but make the effort to understand what is being said. Remember that both meaning and feelings are essential to effective listening. Your purpose is to validate the other person's belief that the issue at hand is important.

- *Nod and respond with encouraging "grunts"*. "Oh!," "Hmmm," "Uh-huh," or "I see," will do just fine. These verbal responses ensure that you are not taking a position on what is being said as well as assure the speaker of your interest in her concerns. Should the talker pause momentarily, perhaps implying that it's now your turn, you should remain silent (or nod your head indicating understanding) until she resumes.

- *Never attempt to evaluate what has been said*. Don't probe for additional information (other than through non-verbal gestures or an "uh-huh" sound) and never attempt to give advice, even when asked to do so. When you refrain from passing judgement, you do not generate defensiveness in the speaker. Rather, you encourage her to become supportive or to look for solutions. Although you do not provide advice, you can occasionally point the way by asking open-ended questions such as *"What do you think we should do about that?"*

The premise underlying nonjudgmental listening is that you not underestimate the talker's ability to solve the problem when given the opportunity to talk long enough about it. If the problem is not solved, there will be no limit on the number of creative alternatives put forward. Your attentive listening is providing the encouragement necessary to enable the speaker to "think out loud".

BEYOND THE BASICS

Beyond the obvious importance of good listening, perhaps the first principle in seeking to influence others is to seek to understand before *you seek to be understood*. (This notion is a central tenet in the work of Stephen Covey, as described in *The Seven Habits of Highly Effective People*, to whom I am indebted for the insight.) Too often we want to rush in to "fix things up" with our good advice rather than taking the time to understand the nature of the difficulty first. We have an instinctive urge to prescribe before we diagnose.

If you want to influence people, regardless of your motive, you must first understand them—their needs, goals, reasons, aspirations, fears and interests. You must listen to them in such a manner that you truly understand their *frame of reference*. And you cannot do that by technique alone. The degree to which you appreciate and practise this fundamental concept is directly proportional to your effectiveness and success in the game.

If I sense that you're seeking to manipulate me with your tactics, I will become closed, defensive and cautious. I will conceal my true feelings, if not misrepresent them, to protect myself from the perceived threat. I will wonder why you're doing what you're doing and what your motives are.

Yet, unless I open up to you and, as a consequence, you better understand me, my unique situation and feelings, you won't know how to counsel me properly. If I perceive that you don't understand me or my concerns, I will likely view anything you say as irrelevant to my circumstances, even though I might benefit from what you would tell me. If you're not affected by my uniqueness, I won't be affected by your advice. *People want to know that you care before they care what you know.*

People filter what they see and hear through their own values, agendas and needs. They listen with the intent to reply rather than understand. They project their own motives onto other's behaviour. Whenever they have "a problem" with someone, their internal filtering mechanism typically responds with *"He just doesn't understand."*

Examine this statement: "I don't understand my daughter. She won't listen to me at all." What's wrong here? If you don't see the problem, read it again. In order to understand anyone, you must listen to them first. It's a simple principle. But it's not easy to reverse our instinctive, habitual tendency to react in accordance with our own sense of what seems "right" under the circumstances. Unfortunately, we seem to want others to understand us and, by implication, accept our viewpoint *before* we make the effort to understand them.

When we listen, we do so at one of five levels. These are (i) ignoring, (ii) pretending to listen, (iii) listening selectively to parts of the conversation, (iv) listening attentively and (v) listening empathically.

EMPATHIC LISTENING

Few of us are inclined to listen at this level unless our own self-interest is the issue. This is listening with the sole intent of understanding the other person. It is a sincere and concentrated effort at listening within her unique frame of reference. The objective is to see the world as she sees it and, at the same time, attempt to understand how she feels about it.

Meaning is personal. We perceive, define and label reality from our unique perspective and for our own special purposes. Our frame of reference is the meaning we ascribe to things, events and people. Seeing a new point of view is, in effect, seeing a new frame of reference. Thinking about things differently is thinking about things in a new frame of reference. Listening to understand is searching for the other person's particular frame of reference—because almost every experience, behaviour and attitude is appropriate given the right context. Only when you discover it can you understand the intended meaning.

Empathic listening is listening with your eyes as well as your ears. It's listening for feeling, for meaning, for behaviour. Instead of projecting your thoughts or assuming his motives, your focus is on receiving and interpreting his message. Your sole purpose in listening is to understand his point of view and his frame of reference.

Next to physical survival, our greatest need as humans is psychological survival. That is the need to be appreciated, to be validated, affirmed and understood as individuals. Just as we need air to breathe, we need "psychological air" to grow. Empathic listening gives others psychological air. Once they've inhaled this rarefied air, they are more willing to listen to our point of view, to consider our options and alternatives and to collaborate on solving problems. They play the game with a motivation to find mutually rewarding, win-win outcomes.

Empathic listening enables you to make the right diagnosis before you endeavour to prescribe the solution. In a sales transaction, for example, the effective seller first endeavours to understand the concerns and needs of the customer. The novice salesperson focuses only on selling the product and thus seeks to emphasize the product's best features. The sales pro, on the other hand, aims at selling solutions to problems (once understood) by extolling the benefits of the product or service to the buyer. *"Diagnose before you prescribe"* is an important skill in the game of life.

When we listen through our own value filters, our replies and reactions take any or all of four forms. We can evaluate (agree or disagree), we can probe (ask questions within our own frame of reference), we can advise (give counsel based on our expertise and experience) or we can interpret (try to "figure them out"). These are natural responses learned over time. But do any of them assist our understanding of others? Do they give people the psychological air necessary to encourage colla-boration? How do you feel when others evaluate your behaviour, play twenty questions, tell you what you *should* do or impute motives to you? Does it encourage you to work with them to find a mutually rewarding solution?

There are four types of empathic response. The first and least effective is to mimic the content of the other's statement. The second is to rephrase the message in your own words—to translate the meaning into your language from theirs. The third is to reflect the feeling of the speaker as well as rephrasing the content. The fourth is to provide the speaker with psychological air, to help him work through his thoughts and feelings by seeking to understand both. Your focus is on more than the issue at hand; it's also on the relationship. The goal is to empower people to deal with the real concern, with you as an ally rather than an adversary.

Empathic communication obviously takes more time than we are accustomed to giving in our daily encounters with people, especially those with whom we disagree. But, on analysis, it probably takes less time than having to deal with the misunderstanding, resentment, and remorse that otherwise arises from the failure to communicate genuinely with others. So think of it as an investment rather than an expenditure of your time.

THE BENEFITS

As you learn how to listen and respond empathically to the other players in the game, you will discover that many of your differences are differences of perception only. You will begin to appreciate the impact that perceptual distortions can have on attitudes, relationships and behaviour. And you will encourage cooperative problem solving in those who oppose your views. Your differences with other people will no longer be barriers to playing the game and finding win-win outcomes. Rather, they will become the basis for real synergy and innovative solutions.

Clearly, the tactical benefits of good listening are many. You get quality information which leads to better decisions and strategic choices. You build trust and become an effective influencer. You not only stimulate better articulation of the issues but also create opportunities to restructure vague ideas into clearer meaning.

Despite your best efforts, how many times have you heard people say (even non-verbally): "*You're not listening to me!*" They were probably right. The key to being a good listener is that you genuinely want to listen, and that requires willpower and discipline. Good listeners are comfortable with silence. They are comfortable "giving over" the communication to others. They listen to the tones. They listen for what is not said. And, as they focus on the act of listening, they listen to themselves.

For most players in the game, listening is simply waiting for the opportunity to start talking again. But those who know how to listen have a real competitive advantage. For they have discovered that the more deeply you listen, the more eloquently people will speak.

6 PLAYER RECOGNITION

Profile the behaviour.

There are a few deceptively simple givens in life. One of them is that people cannot be labelled and categorized for all time. Human beings are flexible creatures. We adapt our behaviour to conform to the dictates and demands, whether perceived or real, of a wide variety of situations and people. Those situations are often complex and fluid. We accept the adage that the only constant in life is change. So what is the value of typecasting behaviour? Because it can make us better, more astute players in the game.

Typecasting serves a strategic purpose in our encounters with the other players, especially with those whom we define as chronically difficult. A typology is a useful device employed in science and other fields of intellectual endeavour. Its purpose is to bring clarity and understanding to complex topics. And human behaviour, while predictable at times, is extraordinarily complex and dynamic.

This "study of types" fits the way we think. The mind is a perceptual, patterning machine and, as such, information is made more intelligible, understandable and memorable when it can be distilled, simplified and reduced to categories.

In typecasting human behaviour, however, we must understand the distinction between stereotypes and prototypes. A stereotype is a fixed, rigid mental construct. It is something that never changes. When we stereotype something, we see what we expect to see...not what is actually before us. So the purpose of typecasting human behaviour is clearly *not* to create or reinforce stereotypes.

A prototype, on the other hand, is a model, usually the first or primary type of its kind. Models, theories, heuristic devices, paradigms and schemas serve a similar purpose: they help us to explain complex phenomena. Indeed, they help us better understand reality. If you want to understand why an ocean liner weighing several thousand tons does not sink under its own weight, you might derive the necessary insights by observing the original prototype of the ocean vessel—a hollowed-out log. The principles are basically the same. Hence, the purpose of a behaviour prototype is simply to generate greater understanding and insight into what the behaviour means, why it might be occurring and what might be done to influence, modify and ultimately change it.

Beyond enhancing our understanding of behaviour, an equally important reason for typecasting is to gain emotional distance. When we apply a label to describe someone's behaviour, however accurate it may seem, we distance ourselves somewhat from that individual. Dealing with others in the first person, as when we call friends and associates by their first names, connotes intimacy, respect and civility. It's easy to like (or to get mad at) Terry, Rachel or Sam. They're real people to you. But what happens when you ascribe each with a negative label, something like "jerk" or "idiot"? When you do this, you've distanced yourself from them and their behaviour. You've discounted them and their impact upon you. "What do you expect from John, anyway? After all, he's a jerk." Somehow this characterization, or typecasting, of John (actually his behaviour) has effectively reduced his negative effect on you.

In a similar manner, as we age, we can have anxiety over unexplained physical symptoms. Once a medical practitioner has attached a label to these new experiences, we can better understand them and take appropriate actions rather than continue to live with the stress of the unknown. We are better able to cope with our emotional responses.

That's precisely the point of labelling the players you will encounter in the game, especially those who might cause you extreme frustration and anxiety. *Typecasting provides us with the insight, understanding and distance we need to make wise strategic choices* in how we will respond to their challenging behaviours. The more we come to understand the type of behaviour we must confront, the better will be our choice of intelligent and appropriate tactics for dealing with, and ultimately changing, the behaviour. An emotional buffer zone is essential to maintaining a rational presence and advancing our interests in the game.

(*A word of caution.* There are some chronic negative behaviours that you should leave in the hands of medical professionals. Indeed, such behaviours and their treatment are protected by the law. I am referring here to alcoholics, drug users and mentally disturbed people, among others, who do require professional help to deal with their illnesses. Do not attempt to either label or diagnose their problems; rather, refer them to those who have the training and competence necessary to treat such dysfunctional behaviours.)

DIFFERENT TYPES

The list of labels that could be used to describe disruptive, unproductive, debilitating, puzzling and otherwise challenging behaviours is almost endless. Here are a few of the possibilities:

Abrupt. Abusive. Aggressive. Avoider. Blamer. Braggart. Buck-Passer. Bully. Chauvinist. Clinging Vine. Clown. Complainer. Compulsive. Coward. Crier. Criticizer. Demander. Denier. Egotist. Explainer. Exploder. Flirt. Gossip. Happy-Face. Hypochondriac. Hysteric. Indifferent. Instigator. Interruptor.

Intimidator. Know-It-All. Liar. Manipulator. Moper. Nag. Nitpicker. Paranoid. Passive. Perfectionist. Pessimist. Pouter. Preacher. Rambler. Saboteur. Silent. Sniper. Stubborn. Super-Agreeable. Unpredictable. Unresponsive. Victim. Worry Wart.

No doubt you can think of other labels. Reflecting on those in your life with whom you must play the game, you may want to make your own list and compare it with those above. Use any label or descriptor you think is appropriate to describe their behaviour.

But this list is not particularly helpful. If there were, as the list suggests, 52 different types of players with whom we must contend in the game of life, then surely we would have to delineate at least 52 different strategies for playing the game. Not an impossible task, perhaps, but one that would require an inordinate amount of effort, time and skill. And few of us would have the patience, let alone the capacity, to understand all the tactical nuances necessary to deal with so many behavioural types.

Fortunately, the task can be simplified. There is a more manageable number, and a more manageable approach, that will enable you to win most of the time. Such is the value of typologies. For example, on closer inspection of the above list, a number of behaviours can be grouped into broader categories that have certain traits in common.

One group (for the sake of simplicity, we will call them *Warriors*) shares attributes that could be defined as overbearing, aggressive and, in some cases, hostile. This common theme is seen in the likes of abrupt and abusive individuals, aggressive manipulators, bullies, chauvinists, demanders, egotists, exploders, intimidators, know-it-alls, preachers and obviously others. (In the profiles of the challenging players which will follow, I examine some of these more aggressive types and provide appropriate insights and tactics for playing their games.)

Another group with like behaviourial characteristics we might subsume under the label *Whiners* (the neat thing about labelling is that you can be as creative or descriptive as you please). This cluster would include blamers, buck-passers, complainers, criers, criticizers, deniers, explainers, gossips, hypochondriacs, nags, nitpickers, passives, perfectionists, pessimists, pouters, victims and so on.

The third generic prototype might be called *Wimps:* the clinging vines, flirts, happy faces, mopers, silent-unresponsives, super-agreeables, etc. Lastly, we have the *Wafflers:* procrastinators, indecisives, vacillators, ramblers, avoiders and indifferents, to name a few. These too will come under our microscope as we examine the really challenging players, their preferred tactics and countermeasures.

The point of this exercise? For starters, four is a much more manageable number of people-handling strategies than is 52, or 75, or however many it takes to play the game. A critically important element in the game is knowing who your opponent is. To effectively influence the other player, you will need to possess the insight, understanding and emotional distance that comes from an analysis of his behavioural profile.

Thus an important rule for survival in the game is to define those essential characteristics which, together, comprise a useful behavioural prototype of your antagonist. The label you choose to apply is not that important (although it does help if it is descriptive of your adversary). What counts is that you focus on the particular behaviour you find puzzling or troublesome and not on the person. In so doing, you will find it much easier to develop appropriate tactics that can influence, modify and possibly change the behaviour to align with your interests and needs.

WHAT ABOUT HYBRIDS?

My research into these four broad prototypes indicates that Warriors outnumber the existence of other types by a wide margin. This may not be surprising. We tend to have our most difficult moments with people who are deliberately confrontational. Their aggressive and sometimes offensive natures logically produce defensive and occasionally even submissive responses on our part. This perception-reaction dynamic is like pouring fuel on a fire. Aggressive people are energized by the defensive behaviour they perceive in others. Beyond that is an innate sense of power and competency that drives Warriors to behave the way they do.

In each of these four basic profiles—Warriors, Whiners, Wimps and Wafflers —we find characteristic tendencies that infuriate and incapacitate us. It is possible to have behavioural hybrids—combinations of these prototypes. Typecasting the players is not a science, simply a necessary rule for playing the game well. People rarely fit neatly into these labels. Nevertheless, the closer the match, the easier will be your task of selecting appropriate responses and countertactics.

As for hybrids, it is possible to encounter waffling Wimps (or wimpish Wafflers) and a Whiner/Waffler would no doubt blame his indecision on others. But a Warrior/Wimp may prove a contradiction in terms. While it may be convenient to suggest that the players with whom you must deal display a variety of these behaviours, devising a label that is not clear or descriptively concise will only serve to make your task more complicated.

Within the broad prototypes used here to demonstrate the typecasting principle, we see the probability of behavioural hybrids and the possibility of player prototypes encompassing seemingly contradictory characteristics. For example, a Know-it-all uses the power of knowledge to bully people. Although not typical of the behavioural profile, your success may depend to a degree on incorporating a few Bully-handling tactics into your strategy. Guerilla Fighters can become Grenades under pressure, exploding into a rage once you've removed their cover. So your approach to the game may require you to select appropriate tactical responses from more than one profile. While hybrids do exist, there are practical reasons why you should endeavour to be as precise as possible in typecasting the opposing player.

Once you understand the basic concept and purpose of typecasting, you will more easily recognize the game being played and thus also which tactical responses are likely to be effective in modifying behaviour and aligning interests. In time, you can choose for yourself which labels are most appropriate for the players in your game.

7 CONFRONTATION

Make them accountable.

Most of us instinctively shy away from confrontation. Yet our ability to handle confrontation and deal effectively with conflict will determine how well we play the game. It also influences the direction, nature and quality of our lives.

All personal renewal and organizational changes begin with confrontation. Pressure groups confront legislators. Employees confront management. Students confront teachers. Change occurs when we confront inadequacy or complacency. New lifestyles encourage confrontation. And the result is usually progress, growth and new beginnings.

Confrontation means facing up to reality. It means "saying it like it is" and dealing with the tangled web of issues, problems, challenges, values, and potentialities that can debilitate relationships and organizational performance. But confrontation is only the beginning of the process. Inevitably, it must lead to a search for innovative ways of solving personal and organizational problems.

Confrontation occurs at different levels of intensity. A disagreement, however trivial, is a confrontation. How often have you observed a mishandled disagreement escalate out of control and eventually end in rage? Knowing how to manage a confrontation and, when necessary, de-escalate its intensity, is a critically important aspect of the game. Without the skills and knowledge required to handle confrontation, constructive win-win outcomes are impossible.

There are at least three types of confrontation. The first involves dealing with the conflict that arises when people hold opposing viewpoints. This is a common occurrence. A second instance of confrontation occurs when we must deal with difficult and unreasonable requests that make us feel awkward, pressured and even guilty. Finally, there are those unavoidable confrontations that ensue whenever we must deal with problem behaviour—when what the other player is doing (or not doing) is causing us a problem.

VIEWPOINT CONFLICT

A confrontation ensues whenever two people hold opposing viewpoints. Even though the issue at hand may be relatively unimportant to the relationship, the normal tendency is to defend the validity of your own view while attacking obvious weaknesses in the other person's position. The result, if not properly managed, can

64

become a bitter emotional encounter.

Consider this example. Fred, your normally amiable associate, confronts you with the following: "You know, I think we ought to get rid of Johnston. He's incompetent." You happen to think otherwise. So how should you disagree with Fred's viewpoint without escalating the inherent conflict in these respective positions? Some people, without thought, might tell Fred that it's none of his business. Although valid, this retort is unlikely to make Fred go away, much less feel good about himself. Rather, it will probably only harden the differences.

Asking for more information ("Why do you feel that way?") is a reasonable response under these circumstances but is also likely to be counterproductive. Unless, of course, you truly want to know. The fact is that you think Johnston is okay. He's a bit slow, perhaps, but in time he'll be right for the job. Therein lies your fundamental disagreement with Fred: he sees it one way, you see it another way. Asking for more information only provides Fred with a soapbox for his views and the opportunity to undermine your position.

To acknowledge honest disagreement without inviting escalation, simply follow these four steps (the first two should be familiar as we've previously examined reflection and valuing):

- reflect the viewpoint that has been expressed;

- value the individual;

- state your position clearly and succinctly; and, finally,

- change the topic.

Let's see how it works. The first thing you do in a confrontation is communicate what you heard the other person say. Reflect back your understanding of his opinion. "Fred, you think we should fire Johnston, right?" This reflective question seeks to confirm your impression of what Fred intended to say. He can now agree or disagree with your interpretation of his comment. And that's the essence of quality communication. "No, that's not what I'm saying at all. I don't want him fired—he's got six kids to feed. I think we should get rid of him by transferring him to our branch office in Edmonton."

Remember, meaning is always in the receiver. A reflective statement verifies the intent of the message and keeps the confrontation focused on the real issues. It also acknowledges the speaker. It says, "I am listening to your opinion and I take your opinion into account before I state mine." Most people are not really seeking agreement from others on every point. What they do want is an acknowledgement of their right to hold a differing opinion. After all, differences of opinion are normal and natural.

If there is hostility in the exchange, a reflective statement can defuse that emotion. This is a logical consequence of hearing that you've been heard and perceiving that an effort has been made to understand your concerns. In other words, reflection brings angry people "down a notch" and, in the process, makes them more willing to listen to your viewpoint.

A word about tone of voice: good reflective statements or questions are usually made or asked in a tentative fashion. It's as if you're thinking as you speak (although you may not be). This apparent indecision, in contrast with a firm or aggressive reaction, implies that you're not counterattacking. Remember that all of you is communicating. Make sure your voice tone reinforces the message you want to deliver. Begin with phrases like, "*I think*" or "*Seems to me...*" or "*Sounds as if....*" Temper your remarks with appropriate qualifications like "*may*," "*possibly*," or "*perhaps*."

Valuing is the second vital step in managing a confrontation. It is essential social cement. It ties the elements together. To value another is to say something like this: "*I can understand why you might feel that way, Fred.*" Or, "*I can appreciate why you would say that.*" It lets the other person know that you value him as a person even though his opinion differs from yours.

Valuing is not agreeing. To agree to something you really disagree with, for the sake of resolving conflict, is suggesting that you compromise your integrity. Valuing simply means you understand that people perceive things in their own unique ways. No two people see reality alike; they see their own versions of that reality. Valuing acknowledges that fact. It says simply, "I heard you and I respect your right to have an opinion that may be different from mine."

Now it's time to state your position. "I think Johnston has some potential, and I'm going to give him more time to prove himself." State your opinion in a direct, candid manner, with an even tone of voice. Resist the temptation to be sarcastic and never defend your position. State it, don't explain it. An explanation invites a counter-argument. What you're really saying to Fred is something like this: "I don't agree, but I think you're okay. So let's exchange our views on this matter pleasantly and comfortably, not as a contest of one-upmanship."

Having stated your opinion, it is advisable to move quickly to a less contentious topic. To wait for a reply to your view is to invite further debate or, worse, to have Fred defend his argument. Moving to another topic says, "We have to disagree. That being over, let's move on to other business." Even an innocuous question ("Have you seen Charlie today?") may be sufficient to avoid further escalation.

Of course, you may not be successful. Fred might persist a while longer, in which case you'll require some additional skills. But focusing on these four steps will go a long way towards ensuring your trivial disagreements remain just that—trivial and not worthy of the emotion required to escalate them to a higher plateau of conflict.

It's time to practise. Imagine that the following statement is directed at you by a colleague and that you disagree with the point of view being expressed. The objective is to indicate your disagreement without escalating the confrontation into a heated exchange you will later regret. Using the four steps just outlined, disagree with this statement: "You people are all the same around here. You're all talk and no action." Think of an appropriate response before reading further.

A good response might be something like this: "You think we don't get too much accomplished around here? (After reflecting her concern, pause for an affirmation or correction of your inferred meaning.) I can appreciate that you might think that, Betty. (Valuing.) We like to get everyone involved in the search for creative solutions. That way we usually end up producing a superior product. (Your point of view.) Incidentally, what did you think of that sales presentation yesterday? (Changing the topic.)"

If your response was different, perhaps you should go back and review the four steps. Remember: reflect, value, state your own view, then change the topic. Practice makes perfect. And constructive outcomes will ensue from formerly difficult confrontations.

REFUSING DIFFICULT REQUESTS

"It's such a worthy cause, how could you possibly refuse?" Ever been on the receiving end of such a request? We all have. Feeling pressured, we give in and grant the request not necessarily because we want to, but because we'll feel guilty if we don't.

But it still doesn't make us feel any better, and now we're angry with ourselves for giving in. Worse, we've reinforced the behaviour and the expectations of the person who made the request, who will thus be back again, only next time probably to ask for more.

Requests such as the one above are obviously difficult to refuse. They put us on the spot and make us feel awkward about ourselves and about our relationships with those who pose these questions. Whatever the intention behind the question, it really is an emotional ploy. Its purpose is to manipulate our self-perceptions and feelings, and therein lies its success. Responding to difficult requests requires an honest appraisal of three things: the intent of the request, our ability to grant it and the consequences of complying.

Can you, realistically, support every worthy cause or grant every reasonable request? You must decide for yourself which causes you can or want to support, as well as what requests you can or want to grant. They may be "reasonable" or "worthy," but that should not be enough to compel your compliance. A number of equally significant factors must be considered—your time, effort, personal resources and preferences. So be honest with yourself. Acknowledge a cause as worthy (or a request as reasonable) and say "No, thanks." That's all you need to say. Don't justify or explain your response and don't attempt to refute the rationale. Either approach will only weaken your position and encourage him to test your resolve further.

Here's another difficult request: "If you really were a friend (you'd grant my request)." Feel the guilt? Now ask yourself: What does friendship really mean? Does it mean that you must grant every wish, each and every time it's made? Of course not. If that were the case, your friends would have the right (if not the power) to make every decision for you. Friendship is based on mutual understanding and respect, and that includes a respect for your right not to grant every request. So acknowledge your friendship first: "*I know we're friends. Good friends in fact. And I value our relationship.*" Then tell him you'd rather not do it.

"You know, he's put in so much time (or effort), it would really be cruel (or insensitive) of you not to buy (or accept)... ." Wow! Another heavy. Refusing to buy or accept something you don't really want is not being unfair, unreasonable or insensitive. Remember, in the case of retail stores, salespeople are paid to sell. So thank them for their attention or service and say "*no.*" Be nice, too. Reward their efforts with a smile.

It's difficult dealing with unknown consequences, persistent demands or feelings of guilt. It may seem easier just to give in rather than face how you will probably feel if you don't grant a request. But think about the consequences. Aren't you just rewarding persistence and well-founded expectations that, ultimately, you won't refuse?

By saying "*no,*" you break this expectation. It's not as unpleasant as you might think. Saying what you feel relieves your own anxiety or feelings of guilt. You will feel good about your own honesty. Over time, it becomes an enjoyable experience.

Summing up, here's my advice. First, be direct. Giving excuses or explanations is always counterproductive. The more you seek to justify your reasons for not granting a wish, the more vulnerable you are to counterarguments. Second, tell the other person how you feel. Expressing your mixed feelings makes it easier for you and more palatable for him; he can now appreciate that it's not an easy decision for you to make. Third, think about what you really want to say. Give yourself permission to delay your decision. Instantaneous replies are often regrettable. Fourth, try, if you can, to restructure the situation to lessen the demands on yourself. You may occasionally find common ground, a third option with which you both feel comfortable. Finally, acknowledge the other person's needs and perceptions. Let him know you understand the reason for his request.

Some people tell me they don't believe responses like these will work. That's understandable. I suggest they at least try them with a sincere effort just to see what happens. Those who genuinely try this approach do discover, in fact, that these responses work. As a result, the challenging players in their lives don't consider them to be such pushovers any more. That is always very satisfying.

There is, of course, another form of resistance to being candid and direct in confronting difficult requests. This one isn't dealt with as easily. Some people tell me they do believe such responses will work (because they've heard others have had success with them) and that they have every intention of using them. But they just can't seem to get started. They succumb to the pressures and later vow *the next time* will be different.

If you are going to try something new, you must make a commitment to yourself. Expecting different results by doing the same thing is, as someone has said, insane. These confrontation tactics do work. The key to their successful execution lies in your willingness to express them. Do it just one time, then observe the results. Feel the satisfaction of a more pleasing outcome, one that aligns more closely to your interests than theirs. You'll not only feel better about yourself, you'll also increase the respect others have for your legitimate rights.

CORRECTING PROBLEM BEHAVIOUR

Some confrontations between players go beyond expressing differences of views or refusing difficult requests. Often the more serious issue at hand is someone's behaviour. It's not what he's thinking that's causing you difficulty. It's what he's doing (or perhaps not doing). In such cases, your objective is to either stop or correct the offending behaviour.

To illustrate, John is in his office trying to concentrate on his budget which must be completed in a couple days. The pressure of his deadline and some missing figures have only added to his stress level. Now the intrusive noise from a radio in the outer office is compounding his anxiety. Normally, the noise wouldn't bother John, but the nature of his task causes him to be easily distracted.

He could close his office door, but he prefers an "open door" so as not to discourage staff who might need to bring urgent business matters to his attention. If it were music playing on the radio, he probably could tune it out. But it's a baseball game and, given the pennant drive, John (also a fan) finds his mind constantly wandering to the outer office. "Damn that Harry! He's such an inconsiderate jerk."

John finally decides that he must deal with Harry but how should he go about it? Clearly, Harry's behaviour is causing him a problem. But if John confronts him incorrectly he won't satisfy his objective: to get the radio turned off without escalating the conflict into an ugly confrontation in the presence of his staff.

Here are four simple steps John can take to correct Harry's annoying be-haviour. First, he must identify the specific behaviour that's causing him the problem. Second, he should value Harry. Third, he has to state the consequences of inaction. Finally, he must encourage problem solving.

When confronted by problem behaviour, tell the other person, as specifically as possible, what it is that's causing the problem. Telling Harry he's an inconsiderate jerk may make you feel better but it doesn't give Harry any useful information about your problem. Worse, you're engaging in character assassination which will only produce a defensive response.

The essence of correcting troublesome behaviour in a constructive manner is to *separate the person from the problem*. "Harry, that radio is causing me a problem. I'm doing some detailed number crunching in my office and this radio keeps distracting me. I just can't get my work done." Now Harry knows the precise nature of the problem. Even though his thoughtless behaviour is an issue, it's less apparent and therefore less likely Harry will become defensive and react.

As noted before, valuing your antagonist is essential to inducing the desired action. It holds together the critical elements of successful confrontation. "I know you're a baseball fan, Harry, and this series with the Tigers is important" (which simply means to Harry, "I can understand why you want to listen to the game"). Understanding is not agreeing. John understands Harry's need to listen to the game; he disagrees with the fact that Harry chooses to do it in the office, especially today.

People need a compelling reason to stop doing whatever it is that causes others a problem. *Consequences prompt people to act.* The more compelling the reason, the more likely we'll act. Harry is unlikely to turn off the radio just because John wants him to turn it off. That is a difference of opinion or, at worst, a values conflict.

Selecting an appropriate, motivating consequence for the other person is therefore critical to achieving your goal. In this regard, the consequences for you are compelling at three levels of intensity: for me, for us (the relationship or the organi-zation) or for you. If you like me, a consequence that negatively affects me can prompt you to take action. If you don't especially care about me, a consequence that affects our relationship (or the larger group of which we are a part) would be more compelling. The ultimate consequence, of course, is the one that either penalizes or sufficiently rewards you. That consequence is hard to ignore.

In the example cited, consider the options available for stating consequences (at each successive level there is a greater motivation for Harry to take some action on John's complaint):

"Harry, if you don't do something about that radio, I'm afraid I won't get finished by quitting time and I'll have to work late. And I promised my son I'd take him to his soccer game tonight." (This is a first level consequence: if Harry cares about John, this would be sufficient leverage before going on to the final step in correcting the offending behaviour. If, on the other hand, Harry is neither concerned nor moved by John's plight then a higher level consequence would be more effective.)

"Harry, if I don't get this work done today, Payroll won't have the figures needed to compute the new pay increases and some people won't get their pay cheques on time." (This is a higher level consequence, one that affects the organization, which of course includes Harry. Failure at this level would lead you to express the ultimate consequence—something that directly penalizes or rewards Harry.)

"Harry, if I can't get this finished by 4:00 p.m., it'll be on your desk and you'll be lucky to get out of here by 11:00 tonight." Harry now gets the message. There's a good reason why he may want to reconsider his behaviour.

A statement describing the consequences can be sufficient in itself to prompt the other person to correct the situation or to appropriately modify his behaviour. In citing a consequence, be concrete. Avoid vague generalizations you cannot back up. Stick to observable facts and deal with measurable units of time, cost, size or importance. The reason for identifying an appropriate consequence is to get the other person involved in the task of generating ideas and solutions to the problem.

Now that you have Harry's interest (his self-interest really) in helping to resolve the situation, you can ask, *What do you think we should do about it?* Your objective is not to impose a solution but to ask for ideas and suggestions. The reason is important. You may find one of his ideas perfectly acceptable. If so, since it's his idea, the likelihood of commitment and follow-through will be much greater.

The use of "we" in the question is intentional. Non-adversarial language is more likely to create an ally rather than an opposer. Initially, the other person may resist by responding, "What do you mean we? It's not my problem; it's yours." But if you persist in using "we" and "our", sooner or later he will use similar phrasing.

The last step in this process is problem solving, which is where you want all of your confrontations to end. Problem solving consists of five basic steps:

- Define the problem

- Generate alternative solutions without judgement

- Select an appropriate alternative

- Implement it

- Monitor and modify the situation (if warranted.)

The problem is defined when you identify the specific behaviour that's causing you difficulty. A statement of consequences provides the necessary motivation for generating alternative solutions. But beware. An alternative which you would both find acceptable is rarely the first one put forward. Indeed, Harry's typical response to John's question, "What do you think we can do about that?" is probably something like, "Why don't you just close your door?"

Remember, problem solving requires you to generate alternatives *without judgement*. If you tell Harry that closing your door is not a good idea, he will argue the point. On the other hand, if you accept the idea as just that, an idea, and defer evaluation until later, Harry may suggest another solution. And then another. The exchange might go something like this:

You: "What do you think we can do about it, Harry?"
Him: "Why don't you just close your door?"
You: "That's one idea. Do you have any others?" (Non-evaluative response)
Him: "Well, I guess I could turn it down a bit."
You: "That might help...but is there anything else we might do?"
Him: "(Opening his desk) I do have a pair of earphones in here somewhere. I suppose I could use those."
You: "Gee Harry, that's great. I'd really appreciate it."

When you depersonalize the problem solving and respond to his suggestions in an attentive and supportive fashion, eventually you will hear a proposal that you can live with. If you don't, and he runs out of alternatives, then (and only then) you can put forward your own ideas. In that case, the selection phase should also involve a definition and discussion of the criteria the solution must meet in order to be acceptable to both parties.

When you finally reach agreement on what alternative to implement, make sure you "contract" with the other person. Don't assume follow-through. Clarify and define the end result you desire. Specify the actions you expect will take place and delineate such matters as when, where, how, with whom, how long, how much and anything else you deem germane to the commitment.

Problem solving without contracting usually means that, before long, the problem arises again. Contracting may require you to negotiate and occasionally make concessions but, in so doing, the commitment to correct offending behaviour is more likely assured. Before leaving each other, agree to what you have agreed; make sure no "fuzzies" exist.

Finally, circumstances do change and good intentions may be difficult to realize. So monitor the situation and be prepared to modify your agreement in the light of unforeseen events. Pursue your objective but be flexible. Establishing a review mechanism during the contracting phase will enable you to monitor the progress of the agreement.

Now it's your turn. Pick a problem situation you've been wanting to correct. Then practise these four steps:

- Identify the specific behaviour

- Value the individual

- State an appropriate (motivating) consequence, and

- Encourage problem solving.

The more you practise these confrontational techniques, the more comfortable (and competent) you will become. And the more you'll appreciate the rules of the game.

8 PERCEPTION & REALITY

You can't play if you don't see the game.

"What you see ain't what you get" is a line made famous years ago by comedian Flip Wilson. That same conventional wisdom applies to managing interpersonal conflict and is frequently the cause of its escalation. If you can't see why people do what they do in difficult situations, you will be ill-equipped to play the game.

Each of us possesses certain coping mechanisms which enable us to maintain our emotional health under pressure. Unfortunately, these same mechanisms can prevent us from seeing, appreciating and objectively analyzing the reasons for escalating conflict. They are barriers that prevent us from receiving messages accurately and responding to them appropriately.

The key to overcoming these perceptual barriers is to resist the temptation to react in an unthinking manner. It might seem that this requires enormous self-control, but it's really not that difficult. (Certainly, a knowledge of your hot buttons is helpful.) The first step is to develop an awareness of the barriers to seeing behaviour objectively. This new-found knowledge will make it easier to *stop and think* under pressure (this may be the ultimate objective in mastering the game of life).

What follows is a partial list of the barriers that impair our ability to respond appropriately in challenging circumstances:

Rationalizations. To rationalize is to justify your behaviour to yourself, to mentally align your performance with your expectations of performance. If you can't say to yourself "*It's OK, I did it because...*", you are soon likely to doubt your self-worth. Rationalizing is what emotionally healthy people do to justify their bad decisions, vent their feelings and make their behaviour acceptable to peers as well as themselves. We all rationalize our actions, because it's preferable to telling ourselves that we're worthless human beings.

How does this instinct to rationalize one's behaviour become a barrier to conflict resolution? Consider the following exchange. You're having a disagreement with a friend over a rather trivial concern: he wants you to join him in visiting a relative, but you would rather do something else together. The argument escalates. After twenty minutes, he shouts "OK! Fine! If that's what you want to do, I'll go! The fact is, I don't really care what we do." On hearing this, what's your immediate response? You're incensed. "What do you mean you don't care! For crying out loud!" (You're shouting.) "What have we been arguing for?" Now *you* are the one escalating the conflict.

Note how his rationalization became a barrier that prevented you from understanding what happened and, accordingly, responding in a more appropriate manner. After all, he just agreed with you. If you had recognized his next comment for what it really was, a way of explaining his decision to himself, you would probably have responded differently: "Thanks. I appreciate that. Perhaps we can visit your family next week."

Once we recognize these barriers, we can respond in much more artful, tactful and intelligent ways. We will begin to stop and think. We will discover how to use conflict to our advantage, rather than becoming its unwitting victim. Let's look at another barrier.

Displacement. Healthy people rid themselves of ugly or painful emotions by venting them. If you cannot do so and you internalize your anger or aggression, the pressure will build below the surface and, like a volcano, erupt at the most inappropriate moment. Unfortunately, people often vent their anger or take out their aggression on a person or an object that is not the cause of their difficulty. They seek a scapegoat to "explain away" their feelings.

Consider this example. At the breakfast table, your eleven-year old son begins to pour maple syrup onto his mound of pancakes. In your judgment, he's using far more than he needs. The syrup cascades over the pancakes and wells up, soup-like, in his plate. He's caught your attention. "Umm, that's enough syrup, Tim." He ignores you and continues pouring.

Your voice rises. "Hey! I said that's enough! That stuff's expensive! Who do you think has to pay for it, anyway? You're *always* taking more than you need!" You've now caught his attention. Still pouring, he replies innocently "Oh. You mean the syrup, Dad?"

Now you've lost it. "Yes! I mean the syrup! Are you having trouble hearing today?!!" Who's escalating the conflict now? Your son now responds. "Gee Dad, it's this container. If only the hole at the top wasn't so large, this wouldn't have happened." Note the scapegoating (in this case, it's a thing not a person). Your son is not the problem; the container is. Unfortunately, by now, you've gone into orbit.

You failed to notice the barrier. It is the mechanism your son uses to get rid of the notion that he might be irresponsible. He's venting the feelings that accompany your assault on his self-esteem by focusing on something other than his poor judgement. He's found a convenient scapegoat to deflect your anger. And your failure to see what's really happening in this encounter only serves to prevent a constructive resolution of the problem.

Role Playing. In life, we all play roles. Whether it be the role of parent, spouse, boss or Little League coach, we act in accordance with our own expectations of how these roles should be performed either because that's how we learned to perform them or because that's how we observed others (known as role models) doing them. We also act out these roles to suit the expectations of those who are affected by them.

Take George, for example. During the day, he's an aggressive union spokes-man. To management, he's a miserable, foul-mouthed hothead, constantly berating their best efforts at finding what they think is a win-win solution to company problems. To his associates on the bargaining team, however, George walks on water, because he wins far more often than he loses. What management finds objectionable, his union colleagues find effective. At night, George performs yet another role, that of a devoted family man and loving parent.

Who is the real George? We may never know, because in each case he's acting out the role—one that is reinforced by the other players. Therein lies another percep-tual barrier: we frequently react to the role and not the person. We fail to recognize that people can act according to who they actually are, who they think they are (their self-image) or who they choose to appear to be in any given situation.

Failing to appreciate the importance of self-image is also a perceptual barrier. Each of us has a self-image that is synthesized from our aspirations, experiences and the evaluations of others. Healthy people seek first to protect this self-image and then to enhance it. Conflicts invariably arise when the latter occurs. When we see people boasting of their accomplishments, for example, or of their heroic role in resolving a difficult situation, we tend to get irritated or angry. (Although we fail to recognize that we are capable of the same thing.)

We may never come to understand "the real person" in our encounters with the other players in the game but, at the least, we ought not become unwitting participants in these role plays. These barriers are overcome only when we have the presence of mind to recognize them.

There are, of course, other barriers that can prevent us from seeing and under-standing how conflict escalates beyond control, especially when the issue is so trivial at the outset. *Repression* is another coping mechanism that can become a perceptual barrier. This one enables us to exclude painful or repugnant feelings from conscious thought by forgetting them. Yet, when others forget, we feel they should have remem-bered. As a consequence, *we* get angry and we energize the conflict. Once again, we become unwitting victims. If, on the other hand, we had the presence of mind to recognize the coping mechanism, we might simply choose to repeat the information which they conveniently forgot (because repetition leads to learning).

Projection occurs when we seek to attribute our own motives to others. We fail to appreciate that, under stress, people may attempt to project their undesirable characteristics onto others. And *reaction formation*, yet another barrier, is a term that describes a process of thinking and acting in ways that are the opposite of strong, unacceptable (and thus repressed) drives.

The purpose here is not to suggest that you must be a psychologist to play the game effectively. Rather, it is to help you appreciate the value of Mr. Wilson's admonition that *what we see ain't necessarily what we get*. Recognizing perceptual barriers (and using them to your advantage), rather than reacting to them thoughtlessly, is an important "rule" to bear in mind as you play the game.

Your ability to use this awareness to further your objectives begins with one simple (albeit sometimes difficult) step: the next time you sense a conflict, *stop and think*. Your reality is perceived. It's what you choose to see. Consider the perceptual barriers that may stand in the way of your seeing what is really happening in the game.

9 PREPARING TO PLAY

Ask the right questions.

The behaviour of others can be puzzling at times. We cannot know either their perceptions or their motives. And the attitudes and actions we view as particularly challenging or frustrating usually differ radically from our own. Nonetheless, we rely on our own value filters to try to explain them.

As noted, the urge to label people can be helpful when it provides us with emotional distance, insight and understanding. But if this labelling is misplaced or undeserved, it can just as easily prevent us from effectively playing the game and influencing more positive behaviour. Labelling someone as "difficult", who is really not, is an all-too-frequent excuse for our own problems or our inability to manage and resolve interpersonal conflicts. Moreover, incorrectly labelling someone who, for whatever reason, chooses to deal with us in an offensive manner is ignoring the reason why he may be our antagonist. Hence, we label people out of convenience simply because we don't know how to deal with them.

Some behaviour is situationally motivated. We can all temporarily act in a manner that is different from the behaviour we usually exhibit. Everyone, at times, does things others find irritating, annoying or difficult to understand. But there are also people whom we rightly regard as chronically difficult. Their offensive and obnoxious behaviour is consistent and pervasive. They treat everyone the same way all of the time. Their manner of dealing with others is not what we would define as reasonable. It's not so much "what they do" that we find troublesome but "how they do it."

Before we get to know the players more intimately, we need some further insights into these puzzling personalities. We will need, for example, to ascertain whether the behaviour we find troublesome, and therefore contrary to our objectives, is situationally motivated or more deeply rooted in their persona. Before we begin the game, we need to be prepared.

To ascertain the nature of our adversary, we must first answer a few basic questions that will force us to look more deeply into our relationship and into possible sources of conflict that may have little to do with our respective personalities. These questions will help us assess our initial perceptions. And, before deciding on an appropriate game plan, we must answer *all* the questions.

THE CRITICAL QUESTIONS

The first question is straightforward: *What is the probable cause of the challenging behaviour?* Many things contribute to problems in relationships, not just conflicting personality styles. The sources of irritation may include a failure to recognize personal values and different points of view as legitimate rights. Not involving others in decision making that may ultimately affect their interests is another potential problem area. Attempts by one person to acquire power, status or economic gain at the expense of another inevitably results in conflict. Misinformation, misperception, miscommunication, unrealized and unfulfilled expectations, or unexplained and precipitous change invariably create tension, anxiety and resistance. In short, many things cause people to exhibit behaviour that runs contrary to our needs.

It is conceivable as well that what you perceive as troublesome behaviour may have, as its source, an unfortunate contributing cause. Unbeknownst to you, your challenging player may have had a minor car accident during rush hour this morning or was informed late last night of the untimely death of a close friend. Or perhaps she lives with an alcoholic or abusive spouse. Such events or circumstances can cause people to deal with you, as well as others, in an uncharacteristically reactionary way. But that doesn't make them chronically difficult.

Consider also that the trouble in your relationship may be you. It's entirely possible that your behaviour (your perceived arrogance, conceit, rationality, bullying or overly passive nature) is causing an annoyingly aggressive or passive response. After all, it takes two to make a relationship functional (or dysfunctional).

Does your antagonist act differently toward others? A chronically difficult person is someone whose obnoxious and offensive behaviour surfaces often and with more than one person. It is not someone who is just "having a bad day" or with whom you may be having a temporary problem or minor disagreement. You must seek to confirm whether the behaviour that's causing you difficulty is also causing a problem for others. If this individual deals with others in a similar fashion, and you are therefore not the only target, then you have discovered an essential piece in the puzzle. Players deserving of the labels we give them behave in a consistent manner most of the time and usually with everyone. Here is an example.

Sharon is an account supervisor for an aggressive marketing firm in search of new clients. In soliciting new accounts, she must develop proposals which audit the weakness of her prospective client's current marketing strategy while making recommendations for correcting those deficiencies. Before presenting them to these targeted prospects, her qualifying reports are reviewed by her boss, Don.

Don is usually quite negative about Sharon's reports but his criticism invariably lacks specificity. "The client won't like it. It'll never work. Do it again." Despite her best efforts, Sharon never seems to please Don. And it's beginning to show. Her confidence is undermined and her ability to come up with creative marketing proposals is increasingly in doubt.

One day, Sharon encounters Don in a corridor conversation with one of her colleagues. She discovers, much to her surprise, that Don's criticisms seem to cover everyone in the organization with equal disfavour. She is not the only target of his verbal abuse. Sharon now has some useful information to help her prepare for the ensuing game with Don.

Are you keeping things in perspective? Probably the toughest question is whether your emotions are sufficiently in check to make a proper diagnosis. I have long been a fan of Murphy. He gave us his laws to remind us what "being human" is all about. For the uninformed, Murphy was the guy who said if something can go wrong, it will go wrong. And when something does go wrong, it always goes wrong at the worst possible time. And so on. (Then there is O'Toole's Corollary: He observed that Murphy was an optimist.) In preparing yourself for the game, it is helpful to remember some or all of Murphy's famous laws.

Perspective is maintaining a balanced view of the situation at hand. It's giving the benefit of the doubt. It's not being too rigid in your expectations of others. It's remembering the icebergs: hidden agendas, double standards, assumptions and rumours. Here is an example of losing perspective.

Your teenage daughter comes to you, in great excitement and anticipation, with her report card in hand. And what a report card it is! The best to date: five A's and one C+. But where, as a judgmental parent with high expectations of performance, are you most likely to begin the conversation? "Gee dear, what happened in History? I know you can do better than that." Sound familiar? Where's your perspective?

What follows is a letter allegedly written by a young woman to her parents following her first lengthy absence from home. (Although I have seen this letter in different variations, the authorship is unknown to me. However, it serves as a classic and powerful example of the difficulty of maintaining perspective. Which is why I have chosen to include it here.) An only child, she had decided to attend university in a city located over 500 miles from her home town. Her parents had helped her pack and had driven her to the campus. Following a tearful goodbye, they then drove home in near silence. Acknowledging their daughter's right and need to be independent, they vowed not to write her until they received her first letter. So, with faith and trepidation, they waited for that initial letter to arrive. Weeks passed. Then months. Finally, after a three month wait, they received the following letter from their daughter:

"Dear Mom and Dad:

It has been three months since I left for university and I am very sorry for not having written you sooner. But you are not to read any further until you are sitting down, okay? I am getting along pretty well now. The skull fracture and concussion I got from jumping out of my residence window when it caught fire shortly after my arrival are pretty well healed. I only spent two weeks in the hospital and now I can see normally. I get these sick headaches only once a day. Fortunately, the fire in the residence and my jump were witnessed by a nearby gas station attendant. He also visited me at the hospital and, since I had nowhere to live because of my burned-out dorm, he was kind enough to invite me to share his apartment. It's really a sub-cellar but it's kind of cute. Although John (his name) is not of our faith or colour, he's a very fine boy and we have fallen deeply in love and are planning on getting married. We haven't set the exact date yet, but it will be before my pregnancy begins to show. Yes, Mom and Dad, I am pregnant. I know how much you are looking forward to being grandparents and I know you will welcome the baby and give it the same love and devotion and tender care you gave me when I was a child. (John is very ambitious, Dad. With the baby on the way, he's decided to return to night school to finish his Grade 10. He's certain that, within a few years, he'll work his way up to night manager at the gas station.) The reason for the delay in our marriage is that John has some kind of infection which prevents us from passing our pre-marital blood test. I carelessly caught it from him. But this should soon clear up with the penicillin injections I am taking daily. Well, now that I have brought you up to date, I want to tell you that there was no fire. I did not have a concussion or a skull fracture. I was not in the hospital. I am not pregnant. I am not engaged and I have no infections. However, I am getting a D in History and an F in Science and I wanted you to see these in their proper perspective."

In the game of life, you can *never* underestimate the importance of keeping things in their proper perspective. Your initial assessment of the other player is an important part of preparing for the game that follows.

Have you addressed the behaviour directly? While most of us know that we affect others in a variety of subtle ways, none of us is completely aware of the degree to which we may affect them. Clearly, very few people really intend to be difficult. The effect they have on others is usually unintentional. And those who are being troublesome in an unintentional way are the easiest to influence.

The antidote to dealing with unintentional behaviour is open, honest and direct communication. Tell them in specific terms how their behaviour is affecting you. They need this information in order to change their ways. Be honest and not judgmental in tone. Your confrontation skills will be useful here.

The more questions you can ask yourself about the person with whom you choose to play the game, before it begins, the greater will be your insight, your understanding and thus also your chances of winning. Before proceeding to the encounter, however, there's one last question you should consider.

Is it really worth the effort? Remember, there is no moral obligation requiring you to work with or even to live with someone who confuses you, frustrates you, diminishes the quality of your existence or who refuses to change his ways. If you sense that you have an obligation to remain, come what may, perhaps you have a victim mentality (a condition that enables you to conveniently rationalize or "explain away" the behaviour with which you must contend). At the least, consider the possibility. If this is not the case and you have done a thorough cost-benefit analysis, then get ready for the game and bear in mind that Rome was not built in a day either.

Prepare for the game by asking the right questions. Know who you're dealing with, whether the behaviour warrants the tactics you plan to use and, above all, whether the game is worth your investment of time and effort.

✧ THE PLAYERS

You now have an understanding of the game, its context and primary objective as well as the barriers that impede your chances of winning. You have also become familiar with the key rules that govern how the game is played. Now it's time to meet the players.

These particular players are among some of the more challenging we'll ever meet. They are the ones most likely to frustrate us, demoralize us and rob us of our capacity to deal productively and harmoniously in relationships. They are the ones who know how to keep us off balance and make us incapable of effective action. They are the ones who cause most of the stress, conflict and sheer wasted time in our lives.

In the following chapters, we will examine 14 of these troublesome players and provide guidelines for developing smart game plans. To be successful, your plan of action must reflect your individual strengths, skills and attitudes. If it doesn't, your strategy will be transparent. In some cases, given the complexity of the behaviour, I will give illustrations of the strategies in action. In these pages, you will discover what you need to know to get your adversaries to modify their behaviour, align with your needs and generally "see it your way." Which is the objective of the game.

What makes these players exceptional is that they are largely immune to our normal methods of communication and persuasion. Having learned early in life that their behaviour is effective in disarming, incapacitating and even punishing others, they have recognized and adapted to the methods that reasonable people use to "get through" to them. Rather than help the situation at hand or advance a mutual cause, our well-intentioned efforts to influence their challenging behaviours usually only succeed in making the situation, and thus often the relationship, worse.

As you become familiar with each of these expert players, note how your tactics and counter-tactics must be adapted to your unique personal strengths and weaknesses. The guidelines and strategies suggested in each case will enable you to create different approaches and opportunities to "get your business done" without the inordinate frustration, anger and confusion that may have characterized your prior relationship.

You will discover that playing the game is learning the game. Done well, it requires an understanding of the why and how of intelligent and artful phrasing of requests for action or improved performance, of employing appropriate non-verbal gestures to support your efforts at modifying the offensive behaviour, and of communicating in a non-defensive manner. Without attention to these important communication skills, your efforts may result in resistance, resentment and revenge.

As you get to know these players, you will create the necessary emotional distance to make good tactical judgements while still living or working effectively with them. With that emotional distance will come greater insight and understanding of the causes of the behaviour, of why it effects you in the way it does, and of how to turn their needs into more harmonious relationships.

Some of these players will be familiar to you. Perhaps it's an uncooperative or overly agreeable subordinate, a pompous know-it-all associate, a vacillating boss or unresponsive teenager. You will learn why your reasoning and pleading with them hasn't worked. You will discover how to become a more powerful but sensitive communicator under pressure. And you will find out how you can constructively take back control of these important relationships.

Are these things really possible? In a word, yes. Provided you are willing to see these challenging and expert players as great teachers. Eleanor Roosevelt once said, "Every time you meet a situation, though you think at the time it's an impossibility and you go through the tortures of the damned, once you have met it and lived through it you find that forever after you are freer than you were before." So it is with the game of life.

You will learn much by observing how your adversaries play their games and how they respond to your newly discovered tactics. You are now familiar with the essential principles and rules of the game. All you require is a knowledge of the tactics which are specific to the needs and vulnerabilities of these intriguing players.

But beware. Each of these players is an expert when the game you're playing is theirs. Good luck!

10 BULLIES

Subdue your enemy without fighting.

Bullies are people who are generally abusive, abrupt, overwhelming, intimidating, and arbitrary with others. Their tone is one of arrogance and their attack is direct, forceful and accusing. Bullies are stimulated by any sign of weakness or submissiveness, and their impatience with people who exhibit these characteristics typically manifests itself in irritation, indignation or even outright anger. They are contemptuous of their victims, considering them weak and overly deferential people who deserve to be pushed around.

Bullies can be very competent and powerful people in their own right. They invariably rise to positions of power and authority. Their self-determined and self-confident natures serve them and their organizations well, especially when single-minded leadership is required. Bullies value things like competence, confidence, social order and aggressiveness in other people. They do tend to get a lot accomplished. But they are also likely to achieve their short-term objectives at the price of creating disagreement, dissension and alienation among those who work with or for them. They neither understand nor appreciate the need for tact, diplomacy, empathy, courtesy and other similar qualities that, for most of us at least, constitute effective interpersonal skills.

Unfortunately, Bullies possess a pressing need to prove, both to themselves and to others, that their view of the world is always right. They have an inflated sense of their own self-importance and superiority. As with all challenging players in the game, it's not so much what they do but how they choose to do it that tends to anger, demoralize or debilitate us. And with Bullies the feeling is often much worse. It's as if you've been run over by a truck!

Bullies appear to derive satisfaction from abusing their victims. While capable of physical assaults, the abuse is more likely to be psychological. They possess an uncanny sense of who will make a good victim. It's as if they have antennae for insecure people, for those with low self-esteem or self-confidence. They seem to know which people are unlikely to retaliate when verbally abused or insulted. As with most of the challenging players in the game, however, it is the victim who energizes the monster by reinforcing the objectionable behaviour with normal but unthinking responses.

How do you play the game with Bullies? How do you get them to understand that you, too, are a human being and that your point of view is legitimate and worthy of being heard, if not respected? First, maintain perspective. It isn't easy. You'll need to be clear about your objectives (make sure they're realistic and realizable), you'll need a game plan (a structure to hold on to when the going gets tough), and you'll need some proven tactical responses.

STAND UP BUT DON'T FIGHT

Sun Tzu, an ancient Chinese military strategist, once said, "The supreme art of war is to subdue the enemy without fighting." Similarly, the essence of playing the game with Bullies is to know how to stand up to them while avoiding a fight. Remember, Bullies value competent, confident, and even aggressive people. In simple terms, they like those people who are much like themselves.

So don't fight. It's tempting, but it's an emotional (v.s. a rational) response. They would probably destroy you in an open battle anyway, much to their satisfaction. After all, who's the *bona fide* Bully? Your primary purpose in this confrontation is to not appear deferential or submissive. If you do, you will only succeed in fulfilling their expectations of your inferiority.

Since Bullies love a good fight, you must execute your strategy with care. Ask yourself whether, or in what ways, this objectionable person could harm you. If it's your boss, you'll want to think before you speak. When you do speak, be somewhat tentative and sincere in your phrasing (because some bosses do have the ability to free up your future, indefinitely) while maintaining a focus on your objective.

If you're responding to a direct accusation or criticism, keep in mind that Bullies are more often right than they are wrong. So distinguish negative from legitimate criticism. Is your performance really always up to expectations? Have you adequately met their performance standards? These preliminary considerations may save some unnecessary embarrassment later. Perspective is reminding ourselves that we can all get better. So don't take it personally and become a martyr to your emotions.

Of course, feelings of fear and confusion are the normal responses to being attacked by a Bully. That's precisely why you need a game plan. Having a plan means you've thought about what you're going to do when certain things happen (perhaps because you've been "here" before). Then you need to focus on the execution of your plan. (When my students express some doubt on this point, I tell them simply to "fake it until you make it." You learn by doing it, not dwelling on it.) When you follow through with the tactics suggested below, things will get better.

SELECT APPROPRIATE TACTICS

It is critical to your success in playing the Bully's game that you choose appropriate language. Use assertive but non-aggressive language. Since Bullies like to control every conversation, they constantly interrupt, whether we're in mid-sentence or mid-word. A simple, non-confrontational counter like, "*You're interrupting me*" (an assertive response) will get their attention and signal your intention to be heard.

What you don't want to say is, "Don't interrupt me" (an aggressive response). That's fighting language for Bullies. Another excellent counter is simply to say unemphatically, "*I disagree.*" With the boss, a little tact goes a long way. So, to express your disagreement, I'd recommend something like this: "*I guess I'll have to disagree with that, Mr. Somers.*"

Never worry about being polite with a Bully. Bullies don't really understand or care about courteous behaviour. Rather, they tend to misconstrue it as submissive behaviour. Your purpose in standing up to a Bully is simply to get into the conversation, to be heard. Use non-verbal signals that command attention, but in a non-adversarial manner. Slow, deliberate moves are best. Always maintain eye contact. Get Bullies to sit down if you can. Don't tell them to do it, just model the desired behaviour (but if they continue to stand, don't remain seated). Standing is the fighting posture and Bullies love to stand. It seems to energize them.

Timing is important. Bullies need time to vent their feelings and run down. On the other hand, you don't want to give them the impression that they can entirely "run the show." So tolerate their initial outburst with supportive non-verbal signals (nodding) and non-directive listening (grunting), then get their attention by shaking your head in the other direction or otherwise signalling your disagreement. Once you're into the conversation, speak from your point of view by using "I" statements. "You" statements are accusatory and adversarial. Something that will energize a Bully.

When Bullies challenge you on your point of view, be firm but don't argue. This difference is essential to your success. You have a right to express your views. Stand up for your legitimate rights. But don't go overboard. The results will surprise you. Because, if you haven't stood up to a Bully before, he or she fully expects that you'll submit to their bullying.

Once you successfully confront a Bully, you are likely to discover that he now wishes to befriend you. This is a typical response when Bullies recognize someone with the self-confidence to deal with them on an equal footing. Having achieved your objective of getting recognition, if not respect, it may also prove somewhat dangerous to disappoint them. It doesn't have to be a lasting friendship.

Bullies are very much "into" power. They tend to perceive and use power in a unique way. They view power as not only what you have but, more important, what "the enemy" thinks you have. Creating the perception of overwhelming power therefore explains much about the intimidating mannerisms of Bullies.

They realize that people are usually afraid of the unknown, that the threat of something is far more terrifying than the thing itself. And, whenever possible, Bullies like to go outside the direct, personal experience of their opponents. They know that people feel uncomfortable and vulnerable when placed in unfamiliar territory. Not surprisingly, that is precisely what they endeavour to do.

Ridicule is of course the Bully's most potent weapon, especially when used on passive and overly agreeable people. Bullies know that if you push a negative criticism hard enough (and deep enough), it'll eventually break down any resistance. Because the more a victim attempts to defend himself, the greater the likelihood that others will suspect some validity lies in the accusation. Bullies always demand accountability. When pressed to do the same, they tend to counterattack with indignation or, in some cases, even rage.

Bullies like to keep the pressure on. One tactic invariably leads to another (because relentless, constant pressure is the best kind of pressure). It's called patient intimidation. In essence, Bullies enjoy power tactics: they know how to make things happen by picking, freezing, personalizing and polarizing their targets.

THE BULLYING BOSS

A bullying boss is an especially difficult person to deal with for obvious reasons: he not only possesses the power of his aggressive personality but also the power of his position within the organization. Employees usually avoid confronting his obnoxious behaviour out of the fear that, "If I stand up and tell him what I really think, I could get fired." So a bullying boss can be an enormously intimidating adversary. (As noted, some games are more challenging than others.)

Marion is fed up and ready to quit her job. More specifically, it's her boss, Sam, with whom she's fed up. While she is quite happy with her responsibilities as junior editor at Atwell Publishing, she's sick of Sam's "pushy and domineering" style. He treats Marion as if she doesn't exist. He expects her (and everyone else for that matter) to feel the same way about things that he does, including topics unrelated to the job. He's never interested in hearing a different opinion on anything.

Whenever Marion's colleagues summon the nerve to disagree with Sam, about anything (including the weather), he dismisses their opinions. He doesn't hesitate to interrupt people when they're talking and Marion has even seen him get up and leave a room while a colleague was trying to make a point. It doesn't help matters that Sam is such a big guy; he was a star football player in college and just about everyone is intimidated by his size, let alone how he treats people.

This morning at the daily production meeting, Jack, the senior editor, was pushed to his limit when Sam insisted that he implement a new scheduling procedure that was, in Jack's opinion, a waste of time and energy. Jack was angry and frustrated. And it showed: "Sam, that's the dumbest thing I've ever heard. That idea could cost us at least a week of work." Marion and the others at the meeting watched Sam's face turn red before he yelled back, "SHUT UP, you idiot. You do it like I want it done or you can get the hell out of here." Then he stormed out of the meeting leaving Jack fuming and the other editors looking down at their notes in an attempt to hide their embarrassment. After a few moments, Jack left. The editors looked incredulously at one other.

Jack did the worst thing he possibly could do with a bullying boss. He raised his voice, implied that Sam was stupid and he did it in front of an audience. In short, he attempted to fight it out. Whenever Bullies feel threatened, they fight back harder. They get mean. They get even. A little blood on the floor causes them no concern. It's just the way it's done.

In order to play the game with his boss, Jack needs a better strategy. The first step is for Jack to listen respectfully to what Sam has to say. When the boss is finished, Jack should reflect back the gist of the message: "So, what you're saying is that we should try a rotating schedule instead of the shift schedule we are currently using?" If Sam interrupts at this point (he likely will): "What? Are you deaf? That's what I just said!", Jack's response should be: "No. I'm not deaf. I want to do the job right and, in order to do it that way, I need to be clear about what you want."

In dealing with a Bully, it is essential that you remain calm. Be persistent and firm about what you want and distance yourself from his nasty comments. Keep in mind that he behaves like that with everybody. So it's not personal. It would be useful as well to identify consequences that may influence the boss. Choose consequences that are important to him, such as those that relate to job performance or productivity.

A calm, firm and assertive message will get Sam's attention. To ensure he still has it, Jack might slowly stand (if Sam is standing). It's appropriate to "stand up" to Sam in as many ways as possible. Jack has another strategic choice to make. He can pursue the topic with Sam in the meeting room, with other members of the staff present, or he can speak to him alone. If he does it with other people present, he must allow Sam to save face in front of his colleagues. Otherwise, Sam could become more dangerous (and perhaps even explode). If he speaks to Sam without an audience, Jack could choose to use slightly more aggressive language. In this situation, given progress thus far, he may be feeling more comfortable with his game tactics.

If Jack decides to address Sam in the staff meeting, he needs to be more tactful: "Sam, I think I can see why you want to do it that way. I wonder if there could be a problem, though. Last week, we discovered that..." At this juncture, Sam will probably interrupt. If so, Jack should use a non-verbal response, raising a friendly palm in Sam's direction and, in a conciliatory tone, say: "Sam. Hang on. I'm just about done. As I was saying, last week we discovered a major flaw in the system."

Jack should continue to describe the problem, raising his palm whenever Sam tries to interrupt. When he's finished, Jack should look directly at Sam, ask for his thoughts and listen attentively. After he's listened to everything the boss has to say, Jack can start over again. It's critical that he listen carefully and openly to what Sam is saying, because Bullies are often right. Jack must be careful not to overlook the benefits in Sam's position.

Although Sam may not be convinced by Jack's opinions, an interesting power shift has occurred. Sam now sees Jack as a worthy adversary, as a person who can stand up to him but do it in a respectful (but not deferential) way.

If Sam refuses to stay in the room while Jack is making his point, Jack must deal with him on a one-to-one basis. Without giving Sam too much time to get away, but enough time to cool down, Jack should approach him in his office. Again, firmly and with direct eye contact, he should say: "Sam, I have to talk to you. It's important and I want to do it now." If Sam interrupts, Jack must respond in a matter of fact fashion: "Sam, you're interrupting me." If Sam accuses or insults Jack, he must respond firmly: "Sam, if you have something to say about my work performance, I need to hear it. But, I am not interested in personal insults or abuse." Jack's primary objective is to stand up to his bullying without engaging in a fight.

Dealing with a Bully who is also your boss requires courage, persistence and self-control. A woman once confided in me that she did not have the courage to deal with her boss on this issue face-to-face. But she was at the end of her rope. She could no longer tolerate his verbal derision and put-downs. She had to do something. And she did. She figured the worst that could happen was that she would lose her job and, under the circumstances, that didn't seem like such a bad thing. So, she typed him the following memo:

Dear Boss: I can no longer tolerate your personal insults and your condescending attitude that all women are stupid. In the future, if you have criticism of my work, I will listen attentively. However, I will no longer stay in the room if you speak to me in an offensive and inappropriate manner. Thank you for you attention to this matter.

She took the memo into her boss' office, handed it to him and left the room. Miraculously (to her anyway), he never said a word about the incident but his behaviour towards her changed almost immediately. She stills works for him two years later and not only has his respect but also the admiration of her colleagues who continue to experience his bullying behaviour.

There is no one formula for dealing with the players you will encounter in the game. To be successful, you must focus on the rules previously outlined. You must do a cost-benefit analysis of the options available. You must pursue your objective with creativity, tact and persistence. And you must find innovative ways to do *"what you normally would not do."*

If your life is plagued by a Bully, you can do something about it. All you need are two things: a framework that will enable you to develop a winning game plan (and that I've just given you) and the motivation to put your plan into action. And that you must find within yourself.

11 BUREAUCRATS

Focus on the objective, not the person.

These are the people we love to hate. And for good reason. I'm not alluding to government officials, although some may warrant inclusion in the category. I'm referring to chronic nit-pickers. We encounter them everywhere. They are the ones who confront us in an officious manner whenever we feel we are an exception to "the rule" or we need a little latitude, flexibility or maybe even some open-mindedness.

The Bureaucrat's response rarely varies. It is reactive, rigid and uncompromising. These are organizational fascists who, paralysed by protocol, seek refuge in paper, policy and procedure, no matter how trivial. Their objective in life is simple— to preserve the status quo. They do so by relying on the written word, tradition, rearview logic and reason. They are impatient with and even fearful of ideas or suggestions that threaten to "rock the boat," labelling them as impractical at best and subversive at worst.

Bureaucrats can wield facts persuasively and can skilfully grasp inconsistencies in opposing viewpoints. They are especially convincing with those who are susceptible, and thus deferential, to their expertise or their position. Their power is derived from and reinforced by their capacity to be rational, inflexible and perfect. Their tactics are aimed at eliminating challenges to authority and negating individual accountability.

Bureaucrats are easily recognized by their favourite, repetitive and unhelpful responses, like "We've never done that before" or "It's against policy." And such creativity blockers as "We've always done it the other way" or "Why change now?" They are more comfortable with words like "maintain" than they are with "innovate." They detest the much-dreaded "hunch."

Decision making is sheer agony to a bureaucrat. Whatever decisions are made must typically result from an inordinate number of studies, memos and meetings that can, if necessary, be recalled (often with supportive notes) to cover their posteriors. Bureaucrats rarely rely on their own judgment. In place of creativity, they prefer whatever worked in the past. They rely on something that already exists which can expeditiously suit their purpose at the moment.

Bureaucrats like to point out flaws in the ideas and proposals of others. They especially delight in detecting an ignorance of "the rules," standards or established procedures. They are quick to challenge and criticize unconventional views as unworkable while holding fast and firm to their own.

PLAYING THEIR GAME

Your success in influencing Bureaucrats, as with all of the players, requires perspective. You need to understand that they are not attacking you personally when they persist in finding fault with what you are doing (or not doing). Their primary interest lies in ensuring that there are no mistakes, either conceptually or in matters of minor detail. They just don't like faults or transgressions against their stereotypical view of what constitutes order. This, then, is their Achilles' heel should your objective be to beat them at their game.

Recognize that these people are not risk-takers. They hate to explore the unknown on the oft chance that something useful might surface and perhaps force them to change their secure and preferred way of doing things. The unfamiliar and the untried threaten their sense of protocol and predictability.

Although most Bureaucrats have a neurotic need to be liked, when threatened, they are prone to play people against one another or to undermine their adversaries. This is really no more than a defensive manoeuvre, but it's one of which you need to be wary.

How *should* you deal with a Bureaucrat? Here are some practical tactics for your consideration:

- *Never give them "final" ideas.* The more risky the idea or proposal, the earlier you must get them involved in the problem-solving process. Broach the concept in its formative stage and anticipate, indeed encourage, suggestions and criticisms. Don't preface the proposal as "new," "radical," or "revolutionary." Rather, diplomatically present the idea as "not too different" or "an extension" of what is currently happening. Comfortable phrasing like "build on our tradition" or "preserve our position in the market" will assuage the Bureaucrat's risk-averse nature and set the necessary foundation and tone for eventual acceptance.

- *Cite higher authorities, third parties and even statistics.* For example, to convince a Bureaucrat of the value of giving up smoking, you might quote confirming data from the Cancer Society—such as smokers account for 70% more heart attacks than non-smokers or smoking is responsible for 83% of today's lung cancer cases. Relying on authority figures or independent sources to support your case will enable you to objectify your argument. Bureaucrats find that both reassuring and convincing.

- *Refer to policy, accepted operating procedures or professional (or moral, etc.) standards.* The attraction of using seemingly objective standards is that they can be presented as your own view of what constitutes acceptable professional behaviour. For example, "You shouldn't hold up this form any longer. You don't want people to think you're unprofessional, do you?" Couching your concern as a standard makes it powerful and persuasive.

- *Just do it.* If you're going to get things done, sometimes (following a judicious cost-benefit analysis) there is no alternative to the *fait accompli* method. Make the decision, accept the responsibility, take the heat if it happens, then forget it. With Bureaucrats, it's easier to apologize with an appropriate explanation than it is to gain their prior permission.

- *Play the paper game.* You may not like it, but a few cover-your-butt memos and phone calls can serve to leave your Bureaucrat defenceless. He might even appreciate your sense of style. Remember that an integral part of your success is to keep copies of everything, simply because Bureaucrats have a passion for wanting to trace the decision path.

- *Think about icebergs.* This is the 90/10 principle. Bureaucrats have mastered the language of "bureaucrateze," which simply means they are capable of using a hundred words when 10 will do. You must therefore be mindful not to get lost in their words. Cut to the heart of the matter and keep them focused on the 10% of the issue that really counts.

- *Use precedents constructively.* Familiarize yourself with examples of successful antecedents and prior solutions. Things that did work in similar situations, albeit perhaps elsewhere. Since you know that the Bureaucrat is innately opposed to risk, don't make your proposition sound risky. Dress up an original idea in plain, old-fashioned brown paper wrapping—something with which he's already familiar or to which he can easily relate.

- *Don't lose your cool.* Never shout, display your annoyance or denigrate a Bureaucrat. You don't want this person to be your adversary. Rather, try a little reverse psychology. Play his game when he accedes to your agenda. Show him how much he is liked when he does what you want. It's really not that difficult. After all, we do occasionally meet deadlines and other bureaucratic necessities. And Bureaucrats do have a need to be liked (because, obviously, most people don't like them).

- *Remember the importance of details.* Balance your innovative proposals and ideas with an appropriate amount of data and minutiae. In the same vein, don't get too future-focused or far-reaching in your predictions. Bureaucrats don't like Blue Sky stuff. Keep them within the more realistic near future. For most Bureaucrats, three months is about enough.

If all of this fails (and I sincerely doubt that it will), you may have to scare him. Feed the Bureaucrat's internal needs by probing the self-doubt that lingers under his compulsive obsession for form, order and appearance. Describing a worst-case scenario is likely to accomplish this objective. This tactic is not quite as nasty as it may at first appear. Ironically, the Bureaucrat may view your calculated terrorism as truthfulness and come to respect you for it. But, once again, keep perspective. Remember the objective and leave your ego gratification aside.

These tactics will enable you to play and win the Bureaucrat's game. Indeed, it is a game that can be easily won provided you do your own job competently (thereby denying him an excuse to criticize) and provided you do not become reliant on him. Because, in a work setting, it's a dependence that could ultimately prove debilitating for your career.

A last word on perspective. Every cloud has a silver lining if you're prepared to look for it. Bureaucrats can provide a useful service in most organizations. They are the reality testers, the voices of sanity in the face of genuinely impractical ideas. So, no matter how difficult your Bureaucrat may become, keep things in proper focus. Do your homework. Be prepared. And keep your eyes open for *his* mistakes.

12 DINOSAURS

Respect the frame of reference.

Dinosaurs are people who live in the past and expect others to do so as well. They are traditionalists in every sense; rejectionists who seek to preserve old values and old ways of doing things. If they are managers, they think Scrooge was a model boss. For them, the old way is the right way. Indeed, it's the only way.

Dinosaurs never question the statements, customs and myths they inherited from their authority figures. They continue to hold and apply these traditional beliefs in relating to the modern world that confronts them, despite rapid change, confusion, complexity and uncertainty. They believe in authority, institutions, formality, structure, security, puritanism, social order, stability, materialism and work for work's sake. Which is why they reject individualism, participation, unconventionality, questioning, equality, change by choice, experimentation and work for self-fulfilment.

Although this Jurassic Park mentality can afflict almost any age group, Dinosaurs are generally the product of another, much earlier generation. For the most part, they predate the nuclear age, civil rights, space exploration, Vietnam, campus protests, ecological concerns, inflation, narcissism and the communications revolution.

While most Dinosaurs arrived on the scene before the Boomers, this isn't a diatribe against seniors. Many were born as recently as the Sixties. (It's not one's age that makes a Dinosaur. Like all the players in the game, it's how they treat others that qualifies them for this behavioural prototype.) Dinosaurs, in general, predate television, penicillin, polio shots, frozen foods, contact lenses, frisbees and the pill. They arrived before compact cars, radar, split atoms, laser beams, credit cards and ballpoint pens; before pantyhose, dishwashers, clothes dryers, colour photography, electric blankets, air conditioners, drip-dry clothing and, of course, before Man walked on the Moon.

Dinosaurs got married first and *then* lived together. During their formative years, you didn't come out of the closet, you put your clothes in them. Banks were open from 10 until 3. They were here before house-husbands, gay rights, computer dating, dual careers and commuter marriages. Before day care centres, group therapy and nursing homes. When they started working, there were no electric typewriters, nor word processors or computers.

Dinosaurs predated yogurt and guys wearing earrings. Time-sharing meant togetherness. A chip was a piece of wood, hardware was metal and software wasn't even a word. "Made in Japan" meant junk and hooking was something thieves did. Cigarette smoking was fashionable. Grass was mowed. Coke was a cold drink. Pot was what you cooked in. AIDS were helpers at the principal's office. For five cents you could ride the streetcar, make a phone call or buy a Pepsi. You could buy a Chevy coupe for less than $1,000 but few could afford one. A pity too, for gasoline was only 11 cents a gallon.

A Dinosaur's value imprinting makes him believe in absolutes—black/white, right/wrong, good/bad and the "way things *should* be." Not surprisingly, Dinosaurs possess a deep sense of commitment and responsibility to their employers, their church, their families and themselves in that order. Success is measured by what one does and by how much one earns in doing it. Beliefs are expressed through maxims such as "cleanliness is next to godliness."

So what's the problem, you ask? There wouldn't be one if they left us alone. These players go out of their way to include us in their game. They are evangelists for the values of a time gone by. They are intrusive and invasive. Their mission is to make other people, especially the younger generation and their subordinates, believe and act as they do. They can be intolerant zealots. They are also, generally speaking, the establishment. Their seniority entitles them to occupy positions of power, authority and responsibility.

DEALING WITH DINOS

You cannot change a Dinosaur. So you have a strategic choice to make: either tolerate them until they become extinct or learn to diminish their impact on you by playing their game. Should you choose the latter option, you will need to discover their Achilles' heel. When that happens, they may begin to listen to your views and perhaps, even occasionally, defer to your judgement. But be patient. These players come around v-e-r-y s-l-o-w-l-y. Here are a few tactics for your consideration.

The first (and most important) thing you must do in playing their game is to listen to them or, at least, appear to be listening...intently hanging onto every word. Practise good attending behaviour. Nod a lot and occasionally grunt in an encouraging manner. (Don't expect them to listen to you because they are not good listeners.)

Many people think that the only way to get ahead is to promote themselves. This is generally true. But not with Dinosaurs. They tend to believe they are brighter, abler and more qualified than others especially those who are younger than they or in subordinate positions. So it's important that you show greater interest in them than in your own needs. Listen to their stories. Laugh at their jokes. Take their advice. (In fact, ask for their advice; they'll respect you even more.) Tolerate their lectures and sermons. Then embellish on their truisms and moralisms.

Since they have a penchant for quoting heroes, mentors and role models long since dead, dig up a few of these witticisms and famous sayings and use them in support of the Dinosaurs' prescriptions for living the good life. They'll be impressed by your knowledge and insight. Because Dinosaurs are impressed by people who are impressed with them. (As always, keep perspective. Dinosaurs can often say things to which you should listen. The tactic of deferential listening usually offers such benefits.) Deference and friendliness, if not courtesy, are critical to influencing Dinosaurs. But be careful not to overdo it. If your attempts at pleasant conversation are not reciprocated, just keep quiet.

Dinosaurs see themselves as good citizens. They value service to others. So it's important you demonstrate your ability to make sacrifices. Defer personal gratification and be a team player. Be respectful of their values but don't come on too strong. Dinosaurs abhor strident and excessive loyalty to any cause.

Although they complain a lot about "the way things are today", curiously, Dinosaurs don't like to hear others complain. If you've got a legitimate beef, be sure to phrase it in a constructive manner. Don't say "Your criticism is not very helpful." Rather, "I would appreciate it if you could give me clearer direction on this. What are your priorities?" is much more effective. Be tactful and be proactive. Complaining is pointless.

On the other hand, should you make a mistake in the presence of a Dinosaur, admit it. Don't explain it (they detest defensiveness). Look him in the eye and say, "I made a mistake and this is what I plan to do to correct the situation ...." Dinosaurs respect people of few words who own up to their errors.

If you want to advance your cause, perhaps in an organizational sense, develop your expertise in an area of interest to the Dinosaur. Never attempt to duplicate his. You want to augment his knowledge, not compete with it. When demonstrating your understanding of an issue, quote third parties as representing your source (Bureaucrats and Dinosaurs may be related in some ways). It'll sound more authoritative than simply expressing your own opinion. Don't say, "I'm a generalist" unless you have at least fifteen years of experience under your belt in that particular field.

Dinosaurs respect people who are deeply committed to their work. Don't say, "It can't be done". Just do it. Resourcefulness, endurance and staying power are valued. Dinosaurs believe you should work harder, not smarter. Any resistance to tough jobs, tedious routines and deadlines would affirm your lack of understanding of the character-building Calvinist work ethic.

When attempting to persuade a Dinosaur, base your argument on their value system rather than your own. You can be assertive but never aggressive. Dinosaurs appreciate reciprocity ("you scratch my back, I'll scratch yours") and things done for the good of the organization, the cause, the church and, of course, the nation. Phrase your requests in these benefit terms and success is likely to follow. If, however, the answer to your proposal happens to be "no", don't challenge it. Simply revisit the subject at another time with a more compelling benefit statement.

SUBTLETIES TO AVOID

Whatever you wear makes a statement. To make a positive impression on Dinosaurs, especially those who occupy positions of power in your organization, your business attire can be important. Dinosaurs resent the trend toward increasingly casual dress in the workplace. What you may define as individuality in your choice of clothes, they call arrogance. To get ahead, be a conservative dresser and save your trendy wardrobe for after hours and weekends. Although the choice is entirely yours, consider the merits of the adage that imitation is the sincerest form of flattery. Remember, it is a game. Weigh your objective against the choices you need to make.

In doubt about what to discuss over lunch with a Dinosaur? Stick to business. Never talk about your personal problems unless invited to do so, which is unlikely in any event. If you must, however, always let him or her know that the situation is well under control. In the workplace, these people have no desire to be your best friend or, worse, your mother. With true friends (or your mother) you can afford to be weak; with Dinosaurs, you must always be strong.

Speaking of weakness, Dinosaurs have no respect for people who get angry or emotional. They admire those who are rational, calm, cool and collected. A sense of humour and joking are appreciated provided it's in good taste. Attacking others for their indiscretions, especially in the company of colleagues, whether in jest or with intent, is seen as a sign of weakness and poor taste.

Since Dinosaurs like structure and hierarchical order, it's important that you know your place in the organization. You must understand and abide by the rules and procedures of the firm. You must know the corporate culture and you must respect authority. This is particularly important for women seeking to advance in the organization. Dinosaurs, both male and female, can be especially tough on them.

As you've noted by now, the Dinosaur's Achilles' heel is *respect*. The more you understand and defer to their beliefs, the more they will respect you. You need not compromise your integrity in the process. Simply remember that Dinosaurs are programmed differently. Their values were imprinted at another time and place.

Respect begets respect and, ultimately, the result is a more harmonious and productive relationship. And there are very few games you can win simply by showing respect.

13 GUERRILLA FIGHTERS

Stay cool and remove the cover.

Guerrilla Fighters are specialists in covert warfare. They prefer to fire from "under cover" which is often thin, if not transparent. These are the cheap-shot artists, the players who use subtle digs and innuendo to make their points rather than engaging in an open, honest and direct confrontation with their adversaries. Like their counterparts on the real battlefields, they are highly skilled and adept at the nuances of guerrilla communication tactics.

Guerrilla Fighters have strong opinions about how others *should* think and act. Their behaviour is passive-aggressive and highly manipulative. Rarely is it just playful teasing. Unlike Bullies who overwhelm their opponents, they prefer to take control of people and situations using tactics that undermine one's self-confidence. They like to hit and run and, accordingly, use the jungles and back alleys of indirect communication. Curiously, the cover they require to inflict damage is usually supplied by their victims who, while they sense the mixed messages in the barbs, don't quite know how to deal with them especially in the presence of others.

Put yourself in this scenario. It is an office meeting and you are the chair-person. You are about ten minutes into your deliberations when the Guerrilla Fighter pipes up, "This has got to be the worst-run meeting I've attended all week." The problem (as always) is that you don't know whether your accuser is serious or just kidding; after all, he's grinning from ear to ear. But, for whatever reason, you do sense the cheap shot. You've been on the receiving end of his zingers before. So, what do you do? The game has begun.

The one thing you never do is to validate the dig by saying something like "Well what do you think we can do to improve it?" That sends a signal of deference and submissiveness. It serves to reinforce the behaviour, energize your adversary and encourage future attacks, especially when he now perceives you to be such an easy target.

A useful counter when the attack is made in the presence of others is to seek their corroboration or denial of the accusation: "Does anyone else see it that way?" If, indeed, there is nothing wrong with the way the meeting is being run, then you've effectively exposed the Guerrilla Fighter. The focus is now on him and his sarcasm, not on you. That is always your number one countertactic: to remove his cover. Make him responsible for his cheap shots. (Should the others agree with his observation, however, your meeting management skills could probably be improved.)

If the snide remark comes from an individual whom you would rather not expose in the presence of his peers—a judicious course of action when it is your superior who is sniping—you may prefer a more diplomatic course of action. In such cases, you might want to offer the attacker a peaceful alternative, without confirming his accusation. To use the meeting example, you might respond to the veiled criticism with something like: "You think we should speed things up a bit?" This is neither an admission of defeat nor surrender—after all, what meeting couldn't be sped up somewhat? But, again, the accountability for the statement now rests where it belongs.

If you're getting the impression that the best way to deal with a Guerrilla Fighter is to tackle him head on, you're right. Only then will he discover that you're not the push-over he thinks you are. Or one of those unfortunate souls who deserve to be picked on. Guerilla Fighters like to play with their prey. Don't let it happen. Always surface the attack. The key question to ask in removing the cover is this: *"That sounded like a cheap shot, Bob. Was it?"* You have to get these players out in the open where you can deal with their attacks directly.

If this kind of response is difficult, even though it is your most effective counter, you might simply look at your attacker in deadpan seriousness and say *"Pardon me?"* Control your body language; a smile or subtle laugh would send the wrong message. When Guerrilla Fighters are forced to repeat their accusations, the humour that masquerades the criticism is difficult to sustain.

But, beware, there is a reason for this label. They are highly skilled in the art of tactical responses. Their favourite reply to your artful attempts to flush them into the open may be something like: "What's the matter? Can't you take a joke?" Or, "We're being a little sensitive today, aren't we?" The smile is still there.

Guerrilla Fighters are very good at this game. They've learned and polished their tactics and counter-responses over a lifetime. Their primary purpose in attacking is to make you feel defensive. They know that, when you become defensive, you will react emotionally. As noted in the rules, you are at your most vulnerable when you are least capable of reacting calmly and rationally. Finding you in an emotional state, the competent Guerrilla Fighter will "take you apart" with his skilled verbal jousting.

Your best counter is to have the presence of mind to anticipate and recognize their tactical response to your initial effort to remove their cover. As with most of these games, bear in mind that you've "been here before". The behaviour shouldn't be a surprise. The difference now is that you're prepared. So don't be laughed off or ignored. Stay focused. Repeat your initial question: "But that did sound like a dig,

Bob. Was it?" Stand up to him without going on the offensive. You don't have to fight to win this game either.

Should a denial be forthcoming, accept it. The objective is not to defeat him. That could have unfavourable consequences. Your purpose is to let him know that you're wise to his abusive tactics and are quite capable of dealing with them. Consider the merits of providing the Guerilla Fighter with a peaceful way out of the confrontation he's created. You may feel like getting even but now is not the time. Keep in mind the sage advice of the Chinese warlord Sun Tzu, "Build your adversary a golden bridge to retreat across."

If the attack has occurred in the presence of colleagues or associates, it may be advisable to seek out the Guerrilla Fighter later for a one-on-one confrontation. Let him know how you feel about his cheap shots and try to surface the problem that may have prompted his attack. There may well be an underlying difficulty in the relationship or a specific incident that has prompted the sarcasm, so ask him to give you more information. Depending upon the accuser and the situation, you might also use this question while still in the group setting: *Could you be more specific, please?*"

ALTERNATIVE APPROACHES

Should you prefer another route, there are a couple of somewhat subversive, but equally effective, tactics you may want to try. You could confront the Guerrilla Fighter in writing. Now that you know the essential question to ask, you might prefer to avoid an emotional face-to-face confrontation by corresponding with him. It's the easier way out and, although not as courageous, it will have some effect.

Another approach, especially when you're not the only member of your organization to feel the slings and arrows, may be to form a "coalition of victims". Team up with other former recipients of the Guerrilla Fighter's venom and make a vow that you're not going to take it any more. In every game, you must consider all appropriate executions for achieving your objective.

Typically, the Guerrilla Fighter's sniping and non-playful teasing are responses to an unheeded or deeper concern. These are passive-aggressive people. They long for power but they lack the skill or the inclination to engage their adversaries in a direct confrontation. Not surprisingly, you often encounter these people in subordinate roles. So develop your counter-strategy with intelligence and sensitivity. The objective should be to channel the behaviour into something more constructive.

In a remedial strategy, you could endeavour to give Guerilla Fighters greater power. This assumes their primary motive is to seek attention. But be sure to assess realistically whether you're not just rewarding their tactics and reinforcing their offensive behaviour.

In dealing with Guerrilla Fighters, your power comes from staying cool. Keep focused on three fundamental points. First, always remove their cover. Second, anticipate and respond appropriately to their normal tactical responses when you do so. Third, never agree with their accusations. As with all the players, an affirmation of their tactics only justifies and reinforces the behaviour.

THE SOLO ARTIST

The easiest Guerrilla Fighter to influence is the one who operates without an audience because the best cover is a group of people who can mask his sarcasm with polite laughter. When the audience is gone, you need to deal with the Guerrilla Fighter one-on-one.

Katy is not looking forward to the monthly luncheon meeting with her long-time friend, Sarah. Katy and Sarah are high-school chums who have kept in touch for almost 20 years, even when they lived at opposite ends of the country. Two years ago, Katy moved to the city where Sarah lives and they decided to meet more regularly.

While Katy looked forward to the lunches at the outset, things have changed. She realizes now why she always felt "bad" about herself after spending time with her old friend. It's not that Sarah is mean, she just has a way of saying things that are hurtful. And, when she says them, she smiles so sweetly it's really hard to challenge her. Katy usually finds herself incapable of saying anything in response to Sarah's subtle put-downs.

After lunch, Katy spends the afternoon reflecting on what Sarah has said. That's when she starts to feel angry. What bothers her as well is that Sarah's behaviour is not new. She has always been like that. In high school, she targeted the other kids more than Katy. While Katy felt sorry for her unfortunate classmates, she was relieved she was not the primary target of Sarah's unkind criticisms.

Often the most difficult step in dealing with Guerrilla Fighters is to recognize their tactics for what they are. Katy, after 20 years, is only now aware of why she feels so badly after she leaves her friend's company. A Guerrilla Fighter can do serious damage to your self-esteem unless you acknowledge what is happening. Now that Katy understands who the other player is, she has a better understanding of the prior dynamics in their relationship. She can now consciously attempt to change her own behaviour in an effort to improve their time together. She can now play the game.

One of Katy's options is to stop seeing Sarah or, at least, reduce the frequency of their lunch meetings. Who needs a friend like that anyway? A cost-benefit analysis would be timely. Katy, however, wishes to sustain this long-time relationship. It is her only lasting high-school friendship and she is prepared to give it the effort. But, since the game is now clear, she will do so on her own terms.

In preparing a strategy for the upcoming lunch meeting, it helps that Katy can anticipate Sarah's wisecracks. She's heard most of them before. For example, it's likely she will say something derogatory about Katy's appearance: "Why Katy...how good to see you again. My word, you look so healthy and robust; if I didn't know you better I'd swear you've put on 10 pounds."

Sarah is accustomed to Katy's normal response: she blushes, looks down at her torso self-consciously and stammers, "Well, yes, maybe a few pounds. You know me, I could never resist dessert." Sarah's digs work because Katy lets them work. A better response would be for Katy to look Sarah in the eye and say firmly, with a smile, "And it's good to see you too, Sarah. You're right, I do feel wonderful these days." No point in using your best tactic right at the start; just deflect the first shot.

This selective response helps Katy ignore the implied criticism that usually devastates her. It may also serve as an underlying message to Sarah ("I'm glad to see you, but I'm not going to be your victim today").

Undoubtedly, Sarah will try again. "Katy, I hope you don't mind but I requested the table over in the corner. It's more private and I know you hate those window tables. Although I've never been able to figure out why you're so worried about the sunlight showing a few wrinkles (she smiles). I think you have a marvellous complexion."

Katy ignores the insinuation. She wants to keep the tone of their encounter friendly. "I appreciate your thoughtfulness, Sarah. That table will be just fine. You're full of compliments today. I love to hear those nice things about my complexion. Thanks."

By now, Sarah may be realizing that her remarks are not eliciting the normal, submissive reaction from her old friend. Time for a more direct assault. Looking at her friend across the table, Sarah asks in a concerned voice: "Gee, Katy, is something wrong? You seem different. Are you having problems at home? Time of the month?"

This is Katy's opportunity to take control of the game. She must now talk directly and candidly to her friend about the real problem. "As a matter of fact, Sarah, there is a problem. I've been doing a lot of thinking about something that has bothered me for a long time. It's very important to me that we deal with the problem. That's why I want to talk to you about it today."

Sarah, having asked the question (and not knowing what is to follow), will initially appear receptive. "You're probably not aware of the kinds of things you say to me. For example, when you make remarks about my weight, I get defensive and when you make remarks about my wrinkles, I feel hurt. I know you don't intend to make me feel that way and I may be overly sensitive about it. But what do you think about what I'm telling you?"

If Sarah really is a Guerrilla Fighter, she will deny Katy's concerns and continue her verbal thrusts, albeit to a lesser degree now that her cover has been removed. Then Katy must make a choice. She can terminate the conversation and, eventually, the relationship. "Sarah, I don't think I'm going to be able to make our date next month. In fact, with my new responsibilities at work, our lunches are going to be pretty difficult from now on."

Alternatively, she can continue to see Sarah but with a game plan designed to modify her offensive behaviour—a strategy built on the tactics outlined earlier. For example, the next time Sarah cracks, "What a lovely dress, Katy. It looks even better on you now than it did when you first wore it four years ago," Katy should ask directly: "Sarah, that sounded like a dig. Was it?" If Sarah responds with her usual comeback: "Gee, you're awfully sensitive today, aren't you?", Katy can simply say: "I pride myself on being sensitive to others. What I want to know, Sarah, is whether your remark about my dress was a cheap shot. Was it?"

Only you can decide how much time and energy you want to invest in continuing a relationship with a Guerrilla Fighter. The good news is that they are more easily influenced than some of the other players. That's because there are a lot of other unsuspecting victims out there waiting to be picked on. But, since they thrive on your discomfort, you have to honestly ask yourself if you really need that kind of aggravation. Or that kind of friendship.

JUNGLE WARFARE

Robert is manager of the records department at the local museum. He is responsible for writing the annual report for presentation to the museum's board which meets in a week's time. This morning, he is working on the final section of an outline of the museum's five-year plan. To complete his work, he needs the updated issue of the corporate "Aims and Objectives" manual. Last month, the museum's executive committee approved some revisions to the manual. The administrative assistant, Mrs. Hoit, who takes care of the museum's financial and record-keeping tasks, was given responsibility for incorporating these changes into the manual.

Robert groans as he thinks about having to approach Mrs. Hoit. He's been delaying his request for the last 30 minutes and has now run out of excuses. "Mrs. Hoit, could I please have the most recent issue of our aims and objectives manual?" With a heavy sigh and a look of disdain, she rolls her eyes, puts aside her calculator and goes to her filing cabinet. "There you are," she says as she tosses it on the desk between them. Robert has one more question. "Has this copy been updated with the executive committee's most recent revisions?" At this, Mrs. Hoit purses her lips, squints her eyes and says sarcastically, "Do you think I'd give it to you if it wasn't?"

Mrs. Hoit is a veteran Guerrilla Fighter. She has the uncanny ability to consistently make her colleagues, as well as her superiors, feel inadequate and foolish. So far, nobody has had the courage, or the skills, to confront her in her game. Like everyone else, Robert needs information from her daily and to alienate Mrs. Hoit, he believes, would be akin to stabbing himself in the back. So, he picks up the revised manual and slinks back to his desk, wishing he could think of something to say that would put Mrs. Hoit in her place, once and for all.

It is difficult to terminate a Guerrilla Fighter's employment solely because of their sneaky tactics and accusatory natures alone. There is little of substance to build a convincing case for dismissal. Therefore, you must find other, more creative and thoughtful solutions. In short, you must play their game.

If Robert really cared about making his relationship with Mrs. Hoit more productive, or felt a moral obligation to help her become more likeable, he might try the direct approach. "Mrs. Hoit, there's something important I'd like to talk to you about. It's been upsetting me for awhile and I want to get it off my chest. I know you don't mean to alienate and frustrate me, but when you make remarks like that, I feel really put down. Demoralized, in fact. After all, I'm only trying to do my job. Just like you are."

If Robert were Mrs. Hoit's boss, he would try something a bit more assertive, but equally direct and honest. "Mrs. Hoit, I appreciate that you are busy. And I don't know what I would do without you. But, I do know that I'm going to have to figure something out. Because if you keep up that tone with me, I will just have to learn to do without you. Now, what were you saying about the revisions to that manual?"

But Robert is Mrs. Hoit's colleague, not her boss. He has no position power and does need information and cooperation from her (though not necessarily her friendship). So, he might try the following: "Mrs. Hoit, I know you are busy and have more important things to do in your job. And I want you to know that I value you as a colleague. I really dislike it, however, when you use that sarcastic tone with me. I'd appreciate it if you saved it for somebody else. Thanks."

Mrs. Hoit may persist, "Well, you know what they say or do you? if you can't take the heat, you should get out of the kitchen. That's good advice for someone with your sensitive temperament, dear boy."

Robert must keep focused on who he's dealing with. He must maintain his composure and distance himself emotionally. He must remind himself that she's deliberately using one of her favourite tactics, an effective counter in this case, and respond firmly with, "Mrs. Hoit, I appreciate your concern. But that sounded like another cheap shot, was it?"

By now, Robert's message should be coming through. He will not be ignored.

He will conduct himself in a professional manner no matter how poorly Mrs. Hoit chooses to behave. Furthermore, any and all personal digs will be confronted politely but firmly.

If, on the other hand, Mrs. Hoit is Robert's boss, he must follow the same game plan. He must remove her cover. But he must do so with intelligence and tact. It will be necessary as well to emphasize a consequence that will reinforce the message. "Mrs. Hoit, I know you are extremely busy and have little time for inconsequential concerns. However, if I am to do my job efficiently, I need your direction and help. When you use a sarcastic tone with me, it doesn't help me do my job better. In fact, it makes it very difficult for me to carry out your orders. Now, is there anything that I could do, or change, to make your job of supervising me easier?" This is an effective way of dealing with Guerrilla Fighters who occupy positions of higher authority.

Guerrilla Fighters require your full cooperation if they are to fulfill their passive-aggressive needs. Somewhere along life's journey, they learned that being open, honest, candid and courteous with people was counterproductive. Too bad. Because they now go through life causing a great deal of unnecessary hurt, frustration and demoralization. Their damage goes beyond those whom they seek to torture, often inadvertently. In the long run, they hurt themselves as well.

Once you discover how to stop energizing the conflict by unwittingly cooperating with Guerrilla Fighters, you will take control of those situations they formerly disrupted. You will not only improve your relationships with them but also your self-esteem.

14 GRENADES

Resistance equals escalation.

Grenades are people who explode, often for no apparent reason. Their explosion is best described as an adult temper tantrum and is not unlike the frustrated and hurting rage seen in children. It is a fearsome attack that seems out of control.

Grenades have learned that rage is a useful defensive and offensive strategy in the game of life. It helps them cope with their fear, helplessness and frustration. It is an equalizing mechanism they can use when they come to the realization that they are without power or, worse, might be wrong.

The important thing to remember in dealing with Grenades is that resistance, intended or not, will invariably cause an escalation in their rage. Unfortunately, resistance is an instinctive response whenever we perceive we are under attack. The primary objective in playing this particular game, however, is to not use force, impose standards or tell them what they *should* or should not do. Rather, success depends on learning to confront their intimidating rage in an appropriate manner, one designed to defuse, not energize, the conflict.

One challenge is that you may find yourself becoming angry in the face of the Grenade's onslaught. Expect this emotional response but don't become its victim. Feelings of fear and confusion are also natural and appropriate reactions when under attack. As hard as it may seem, your success in dealing with these exploders will be directly proportional to your ability to get your own emotions under control. Only then can you utilize some proven tactics to get their tantrums in check.

Since anger must be vented, your game strategy must be to let the Grenade's energy level run down. You need to get them "down" to a more rational level of inter-action, to the point where they can consider the consequences of their behaviour. While your purpose is to wait them out (without losing your cool in the process), you can't wait too long. Otherwise, they may come to feel justified in their attack on you. Consider your timing. At some point, you must get into the conversation.

You need to get their attention and then confront their rage in a non-threatening way. Use the broken-record technique by acknowledging repetitively (both verbally and non-verbally): "Yes. Yes. Yes." If that doesn't work, say "Excuse me." and repeat the phrase until he stops to lets you speak. Your non-verbal gestures should command attention without appearing to be overly aggressive. Make slow, deliberate gestures rather than quick, darting movements which could be construed as attacking. The objective at this early stage of the game is simply to get into the conversation after they've vented some of their anger.

Next, you need to acknowledge the seriousness of their concerns. Some validation is necessary to assure them that their explosion has had an impact. "This is obviously important to you, Sandy, and I do want to discuss it with you...but not this way." Continue to validate their feelings: "I can see you're really angry about this. I want to help. But when you yell at me, there's not much I can do."

As indicated, resistance equals escalation, so never say "Calm down!" Rather, confront the rage intelligently and appropriately. Use your confrontation skills to deal with the irrational behaviour. Break the issue down into more manageable proportions. If necessary, provide some time (or distance) separation to enable the Grenade to regain his self-control.

There are more sophisticated techniques which will require some practice. Forced rational decision making is a process used by crisis mediators adept in dealing with high-risk situations, such as hostage negotiations. But it works just as well with exploders who, like children, tend to throw temper tantrums. In simple terms, this tactic involves giving the Grenade critical choices while keeping in mind her inability to make such decisions—largely because the emotional intensity makes her incapable of appreciating the consequences. Once the consequences of the irrational behaviour have been spelled out, a skilled crisis negotiator usually makes the right choice for the Grenade. A series of such forced choices over time enables venting and, assuming good choices are made, the building of trust between the antagonists. Eventually, exploders are able to distinguish for themselves the importance of positive choices and the attendant consequences of making poor choices.

AN INTIMATE GRENADE

Christine and Nick have been married for ten years and have two young children. Nick is the CEO of a thriving computer software company and Christine is a consultant with the local school board. This couple would both be described as intelligent, sociable and aggressive by their colleagues and friends. Nick, in particular, is an extremely self-confident and ambitious guy. Christine and others who know him well would say he is a workaholic.

There is no doubt in Christine's mind that Nick is a bit of a Bully. In fact, that was one of the reasons she was attracted to him in the first place. His confidence and ability to push his ideas forward reminded her of her father. Since she had always known how to deal effectively with her father, she thought she could deal with Nick's occasional tirades. While others might have had difficulty with Nick's aggressive streaks, Christine understood the best way to deal with him was not to fight. Most of the time this worked.

Every once in a while, however, something would trigger Nick's temper and his bullying turned into a frightening explosion. After ten years of married life, Christine knew his hot buttons. Normally, a cool-headed and controlled person, he could explode into an unpredictable yelling frenzy. At first, Christine responded by yelling back. Fight fire with fire, she thought. Slowly, she came to understand that this approach only energized Nick. Indeed, some of their verbal battles had come perilously close to being physical.

After several years of infrequent but upsetting scenes, Christine decided that a more rational approach to this game might be in order. Their next confrontation occurred in an airport parking lot. After a long flight, Christine offered to drive home because she thought Nick had had "too much" to drink on the trip. When Nick (who preferred to drive) refused, she became adamant and insisted that she drive, particularly as it was her car. She deliberately kept her voice calm and her words diplomatic as Nick's voice started to rise. When Nick commanded her to get into the car "or else", she gave him the keys. She knew he would likely use force to get them from her anyway. Then she told him, calmly but firmly, that he could drive himself home. She would find another way to get there. Which she did. When Christine eventually arrived by airport limousine, Nick greeted her with, "I hope you're satisfied."

This is a good example of how some spouses can bring out the worst in each other. Especially when they don't recognize the game being played. Challenging behaviour is often situational. The majority of Nick's business acquaintances see him as a Bully, not as a Grenade. It would not occur to them that this controlled and supremely confident person would ever explode. But Christine knows that a Bully can become a Grenade when confronted by an "overload" situation. When Nick's hot buttons are pressed (particularly by loved ones), he can suffer emotional overload and lose control. When emotion enters the picture, self-control often goes out the window.

Christine should also take a good look at her own behaviour and what it is she does to unwittingly fuel the explosion. It takes two to play the game. When she discovers herself in the midst of one of Nick's tantrums, she must learn to maintain her composure rather than energize the situation by yelling back or, worse, using physical force (such as throwing objects). On the other hand, by remaining too calm and rational, she risks becoming a victim and, in the process, legitimizing his anger.

When Grenades are "under the influence" of either alcohol (as Nick probably was after the long flight) or drugs, it is advisable to leave the scene of the confrontation. The immediate objective is to bring the exploder under control, to help him move from his state of irrationality to one of more rational thought. Anyone whose brain is affected by chemicals will be unaffected by even your best tactics. Save your game plan for another time when the exploder is able to understand consequences.

Christine's tactic of leaving the scene of the encounter worked this time but it probably did little to improve their relationship. She will learn from her experience, however. Several days later, when things return to normal, she can talk to Nick about their altercation and her feelings in the airport parking lot. She will present the issue to Nick as a problem to be solved mutually: "I don't mind you drinking on the flight. I do mind that you insist on driving us both home when you have been drinking. I feel this is unfair to me. How can we handle this next time so that we don't have the same kind of ugly situation?"

Christine knows how to play the game with Nick when he is rational. She didn't have the time to think through her strategy when he exploded. To deal with her Grenade, she needs to reflect upon why he is being irrational. Perhaps he is feeling misunderstood or is overloaded with other concerns of which she is unaware. Maybe he doesn't expect his wife to be the aggressor. She needs to realize as well that yelling back at Nick won't work. It will just make him angrier. She needs to use appropriate tactics that help Nick to regain his composure. Letting him "wind down" appears to be effective. She has discovered that letting him know she is listening and understanding does get his attention. She is learning to play his game rather than fighting his offensive behaviour.

EXPLODING BOSSES

Mary is the dental assistant to Tom Bridge, a prominent dental surgeon, much respected and well-liked by his patients. The problem is that Dr. Bridge is a Grenade. With his patients, he is able to keep it under control, usually venting his frustration in silence (although he occasionally throws his instruments instead of yelling). Mary has held her job for about three months and, except for this problem, is quite happy. The rest of the staff have told her that dental assistants "usually last about six months" because of his temper tantrums. Since Ventura is a small town, there aren't many good jobs in Mary's field. And, as a single parent, she is not interested in moving her family to find a new job. She knows she has to discover a way to deal with Dr. Bridge.

Mary has noticed that his outbursts are more apt to occur towards month end when he is preoccupied with updating the books and meeting with his accountant. This analysis of the situation prepares her to emotionally distance herself from the encounter she knows is inevitable. Fortunately, she knows she is not the problem; it would be counterproductive to take it personally. Nonetheless, she wonders to what extent she might be one of the reasons for his outbursts. When a dentist is in the middle of a tricky and delicate procedure and is accustomed to a seasoned assistant anticipating his needs, a new employee's hesitation or ignorance of the dentist's unique operating manner might be a major source of his frustration.

It might be useful to speak to other members of Dr. Bridge's staff to collect information about his procedures and preferred operating style. Whenever an explosion does occur, she might go soon afterwards and ask for feedback on improving her work. Tact is important but firmness and persistence will advance her objective. "Dr. Bridge, I'm concerned about what happened during the last appointment. I sensed, when you threw the probe, you were frustrated with me. I want to do a good job and I need to know how to improve. Throwing an instrument after I give it to you doesn't give me the information I need. What can I do to make your job easier?"

This technique is called "negative inquiry." Its purpose is to gather specific information. Mary will listen to what he says, reflect back the important points and, when he's finished, ask, "Is there anything else?" Most bosses, including Grenades, will be pleasantly surprised to hear from an employee who is so genuinely interested in their continuous improvement. After Dr. Bridge's advice is given, Mary might offer some suggestions of her own: "Dr. Bridge, your ideas are helpful. Thank you. In order for me to successfully carry them out, this is what I need from you." Now it is Mary's turn to clearly express her expectations about what she needs in order to do her job effectively and, in this case, about how she wants (or doesn't want) to be treated. "When you throw instruments, it scares me and I can't think clearly. It makes it more difficult for me to do my job well. If I'm going to be the best assistant you've ever had, then I need you to tell me that you're angry or frustrated."

If, after employing this tactic, Dr. Bridge continues with his tantrums, Mary will need to try a different approach. After all, success in the game of life is all about making the right strategic choices. Since dental assistants are not in abundant supply in the town of Ventura, she might try identifying an appropriate consequence: "Dr. Bridge, we have a choice as I see it. You can tell me what you need and I will get the job done. If you are angry with me, you can tell me that too. However, if you throw instruments at me, I will have to leave the room. I don't want to get hurt." Then she must follow through with her plan.

EMOTIONAL TRIGGERS

You may find that your Grenade uses profanity in his tirade. This is not uncommon. Rather than focusing on the words you hear, as upsetting as they might be, it will be more constructive to your ultimate purpose to deal with the emotion behind them. In some cases, Grenades use such language to deliberately prompt a reaction. Or it may be an unfortunate habit. In any event, you will only fuel the rage if you react specifically to the inappropriate language. Instead, focus your tactics on defusing his anger and bringing him "down" to a more rational plateau. When he is calmer, you can then talk to him about his language, if that is important to you.

People often say things they don't mean, especially in the heat of an emotional encounter. In most cases, it is more constructive to ignore it. But if you choose to deal with it, you might say something like: "I know you get frustrated and need to yell at me. I can usually handle that. But when you use words like (expletive), I feel hurt and insulted. Then I just don't listen to what you're really trying to tell me. I get caught up in all that foul language. So the next time you use those words in my presence, I will have to leave the room (or hang up the phone)."

As you become more familiar with your Grenade's behavioural profile, you will begin to recognize certain signals that indicate an explosion is imminent. That may be the time to back off (if you are pushing a hot button), listen more attentively (if his explosion is triggered by some frustration in trying to communicate with you) or simply change the subject. You can decide to play the game another time.

As always, remember the importance of perspective. Anger and hostility are often in the eye of the beholder.

15 KNOW-IT-ALLS

Make them think.

We all value expertise but dealing with experts who think they "know it all" can be a humiliating and debilitating experience. Experts are of course highly productive people and necessary to our way of life, especially when they use their knowledge to the benefit of humankind.

Know-it-alls, on the other hand, believe they know everything there is to know and therefore that other viewpoints don't really count. Their arrogance and conceit in their self-knowledge causes them to speak with absolute certainty, thus leaving the people around them feeling inept, confused or stupid. As with all challenging people, it's their behaviour we find obnoxious and offensive. It's how they choose to treat others who have less knowledge than do they. It's their demeaning, rejecting and devaluing style.

The dilemma in learning how to play the game with Know-it-alls is to appreciate that they do know a great deal. They are quite thorough and accurate and their opinions usually turn out to be right. But their approach to giving advice, especially in group settings, leaves little room for the judgment, creativity and resourcefulness of others. Their pompous behaviour, more often than not, tends to make those around them feel unneeded, if not useless.

None of us wants or needs to be robbed of our identity, dignity or self-respect. Yet few egos, fragile as they are, can withstand the onslaught of a self-righteous Know-it-all. These are highly insistent people, bolstered by the incredible power of their accumulated knowledge, whose essential purpose in life, it seems, is to convince you that they're always right...and, by implication, that you're always wrong.

How do you defend yourself from an attack or, better still, modify the caustic behaviour of Know-it-alls? You start by realizing that you too know a great deal. The sum of the accumulated life experiences, learning and observations of the average adult is estimated to be equivalent to about 15,000 encyclopaedic volumes of information. Whether or not you spent several years in an undergraduate or graduate institution of learning, as did most Know-it-alls, you nonetheless spent the same amount of time interacting in the real world, accumulating the wisdom that flows from your own hard knocks, trials and attendant errors. In other words, your life experience is useful knowledge when applied in the right ways.

115

We all know people who are intellectually brilliant but who lack common sense. Some would argue that the narrow focus and epistemological rigidity that accompanies higher education constitute barriers to creative thought. What counts in life is not how much we know but how we configure the knowledge we possess and how we apply it to the task at hand. Often a fresh pair of eyes, or innocent words from the "mouths of babes" provide the insight necessary to conquer monumental tasks.

Your best defence to the Know-it-all's arrogant onslaught is a strong sense of self-esteem—a belief in your own abilities and the uniqueness of your own point of view. Value imprinting dictates that no two people ever see anything in quite the same way. Differences of viewpoint, whether based on perceptual distortions, biases or differences of fact, are unavoidable. The object is to be flexible and open-minded, to seek to understand these different points of view and to profit from them. Know-it-alls, unfortunately, are neither flexible nor open-minded. But that should not lead you to doubt the validity and value of your own unique way of perceiving problems and solutions. That premise is the foundation of your game plan.

PLAYING THE GAME

Know-it-alls are energized by any assault upon their expertise. Having mastered the art of verbal jousting, semantic counter-punches and repartee, they relish a good battle of wits. Losing such an encounter would be a serious blow to their intellectual pride. Even when they appear to be losing the argument, they have the verbal skill to tie you up in semantic knots. So, at all costs, try to avoid direct challenges to their authority or knowledge.

A successful game plan relies upon subtlety. The objective is to underwhelm not overwhelm your adversary. It is vital to your success that you not argue with the Know-it-all. Rather, you should present your views as suggestions, proposals and "what ifs." Always present your viewpoint as an alternative: "You know, that's really interesting, Chris. And another way of looking at it is...."

Should you choose to take on a Know-it-all, be prepared. Do your homework. You will be disregarded and rapidly dismissed if you don't know what you are talking about or are inaccurate. Worse, you may cause your adversary to "play with" and make fun of you in the presence of others. Also, more often than not, you will be the last to know. To be successful in any game, recognize the strengths of your adversary and plan accordingly.

If Know-it-alls have a weakness, it is a strong desire for recognition of their expertise. To influence Know-it-alls, it is advisable to first demonstrate your respect for their knowledge. Validate their feelings: "Mary, it sounds like you've done a lot of research on this." Resist the natural temptation to disagree non-verbally. Don't send a mixed message. Be sincere: listen, reflect and acknowledge the Know-it-all's competence. (It's possible that you will learn something.) Your perceived respect for their opinions will be rewarded with less verbiage. That, in itself, will be a small victory—a signal that your tactics are working.

Learn how to question Know-it-alls without confrontation or implied aggressiveness. The last thing you want to do is create the impression that you are also an expert on the topic under discussion. So lead in tentatively: "I'm having some trouble with that point, Gord. Could you please explain it again."

The best tactic is to ask questions that actually make them think or that force them to delve more deeply into their expertise to find an answer. These are sequential (or extensional) questions. Even real experts find these questions difficult to answer.

An expert is one who is capable of answering virtually any question within her sphere of competence. Experts are the people we consult when we need to know the consequences to a *"what would happen if..."* question. Rarely, however, have experts fathomed the sequences to the consequences of the question, as in: *"If that happens, what will happen in six months?"* This is the sort of question that requires both legitimate experts and Know-it-alls alike to actually think, as opposed to reacting with their usual cocksure confidence. (After all, even experts can't accurately foretell the future.) And that's when you, as a thinking human being with your own views on the topic, will have made an impression. You will have engendered a new respect for your views. You may have also won the game.

WINDBAGS

These people play a different game but one that sounds a lot like Know-it-alls. Windbags are phoney experts who really don't know a great deal about the topic, even though they may sound like they do.

Windbags are like Know-it-alls in many ways. They too get angry and irritated when you don't see it exactly their way. The primary difference is that, while they speak with the same absolute certainty as Know-it-alls, they actually turn out to be wrong or misleading most of the time.

The frustration they can cause us depends on who they are. In the process of seeking to convince them of the errors in their diatribe, we are typically left feeling frustrated or even angry about the fact that, once again, we were "sucked in" by their apparent mastery of the subject.

Windbags are basically insecure people who seek the admiration, approval or affection of others. They acquire bits and pieces of knowledge from the media or from gossip but rarely, if ever, do they take the time necessary for in-depth understanding.

They never do their homework. Like Know-it-alls, they speak forcefully with self-assured confidence and frequently become annoyed and even hostile when others disagree with their nonsensical conclusions. Normally, they are just simple nuisances. But when they occupy positions of importance in our lives (like relatives and business partners), they can create a great deal of resentment and confusion.

Here are four suggestions for dealing with Windbags. First, do your homework. You may not be right either. Second, state the facts (as you understand them) as an alternative viewpoint and therefore not the only version. Third, give them a peaceful way out. Allow them to save face by gracefully changing the topic. "That's really interesting, Harry. I never quite thought of it that way before. By the way, what did you think about Lou's management report today?" There's no real advantage to proving them wrong (unless you want to be a Know-it-all). Fourth, you might write them a diplomatic note after the encounter outlining your views and supporting them by reference to authoritative sources.

Never argue with Know-it-alls or Windbags. You can't win. They both love to argue and they won't change their point of view regardless of how good or valid your counterargument might be. Instead, be creative, find a way to be heard, then move on to other, more constructive topics.

16 MANIPULATORS

Establish the rules.

Manipulators are challenging people who use deceptive behaviour to get what they want from others. Creative and cunning, they are adept at devising nefarious strategies and options for playing their "I win, you lose" game. They don't especially care if others get what they need so long as, when all is said and done, they are left holding exactly what they want.

Manipulators believe that others "owe them." Their credo is "screw them before they screw you." Life is basically unfair and charity begins at home. They discovered early on that you could get a lot more out of life by being clever rather than being honest. These are people who prefer getting even to getting angry with others.

For Manipulators, relationships are strictly utilitarian—they are useful for whatever they can provide. Relationships are a way to accumulate power by aligning with influential or important people (those who can give them what they want). Not surprisingly, they like to keep score to compare their possessions to those of others. They rarely trust other people, because they assume (like them) everyone is out to line his pockets at the expense of others. If life is one big bowl of cherries, their game is to eat yours, then grab theirs, before anyone can beat you to it.

As a result of this adversarial thinking, Manipulators don't take the time necessary to understand other points of view. They lack empathy, especially for those whom they perceive to be different from themselves. They are extremely disciplined, able to hide or disguise their feelings from others when it suits their purpose. When they become angry, they know the value of being passively aggressive. They have learned that silence is more effective than rage. They can lie easily. And they know how to be resentful. After all, resentment justifies their deceptive behaviour.

Manipulators are cautious, coy and distrustful. They like to devise strategies, play games, bargain and compromise. They approach their game in a very logical and specific way. They are expert players. They typically think through all the moves before making any of their own. In fact, they would prefer to have all the pieces before the game even begins.

Since everything about their game is so premeditated, they are not good at abstract thought. They are literalists. So their weakness in strategic situations is a tendency to make snap judgments without thinking through the alternatives. Their predisposition to win-lose outcomes also impairs their ability to see synergistic, win-win scenarios.

Their favourite tactics are acting confused or stupid, playing the martyr or acting helpless, pitting people against one another, and trading "favours." They believe in the adage that dumb can be smart. They are usually charming people who know the value of being dramatic when the occasion warrants. In chameleon-like fashion, they can become blamers, pleaders and pretenders.

Manipulators like the notion of rational compromise. They are big on reciprocity and support the notion of "you scratch my back, I'll scratch yours" (and then you'll owe me another one!). That is the preferred option after they've tried to con you and failed. Because, if their strategy to get it all doesn't work, they will bargain for half. But never less than half. Then they'll try again for the other half. In business, they are always looking for the competitive advantage.

CLEVER USE OF INFLUENCE

Like all of us, Manipulators have certain fears and needs. Your ability to understand and align with these needs is the essence of playing their game. Manipulators are afraid of not getting their full and fair share, which they believe they are entitled to receive. They fear being cheated and not "measuring up" to the competition. Their overriding concern that someone may some day even up the score gives them a heightened sense of justice, as well as paranoia. As a result, they think other people are attempting to take advantage of them. This may not be surprising, because the more they acquire, the more they must defend. In time, their possessions end up owning them. And their paranoia serves to turn potential allies into adversaries.

To deal effectively with Manipulators, you must focus on the process, not the substance, of the encounter. You must ensure you understand the rules of their game before proceeding. Better still, you should endeavour to establish them. Your purpose in attending to these ground rules is twofold. First, Manipulators love to change the rules (consider it a preferred tactic). Second, when the rules are clear and firm, Manipulators allow themselves to be more trusting and thus less deceptive.

Confront their deception head on. Being coy or polite is pointless. Ask them to verify their facts, their promises and their authority. Insist on fair criteria, standards or procedures. Should they act offended by your bluntness and candour, say you trust them but that's just how you prefer to do business. Make it clear that you don't want any misunderstandings later. "I assume you're telling me the truth and therefore that you won't mind explaining this to me. I need to understand exactly how you arrived at these figures."

Manipulators are masters of verbal confusion. They like to ramble, go in circles, use gobbledegook and introduce irrelevant issues. Don't let it happen. Interrupt them. Ask them to explain. Tell them you're confused. Summarize or paraphrase what you've just heard and then refocus the conversation on the real issues. Ask them to help you understand the point they're trying to make. "What I hear you saying is.... But I'm not sure I understand what that has to do with our problem. Can you help me with this?"

Some Manipulators like to sulk and use the silent, unresponsive treatment. It's the tactic of passive aggression. The best counter is to make the tactic explicit. "Let me know when you would like to talk, Harold. In the meantime, I have other things to do." Don't reward or reinforce this sort of behaviour. The unspoken message is that "You can pout as long as you want. It certainly won't result in getting you what you want from me."

Alternatively, you can bring the real issue to the surface by asking a series of pertinent questions. Ask them specifically to explain their concerns or verify their position. Should they counter with an accusation (a typical manoeuvre), resist the normal tendency to become defensive. Calmly acknowledge that there may be some truth in their accusation (whether there is or not is irrelevant), then ask them to verify their facts. Don't get sidetracked from the real issues. Simply refuse to play their game.

Manipulators like to use logic to convince you that they are right and you are wrong. They ask a lot of rhetorical and "why" questions, often in an accusing tone, to back you into a defensive shell. "Well, if you really didn't have anything to hide, you would have told me everything. Wouldn't you?" Don't take the bait. You would only be reacting to the tone or trigger words in their questions. Stay calm and keep focused. While logic is a form of argument; some logical conclusions can be nonsensical.

The Manipulator's well-developed skill of verbal jousting can often enable him to slip away from accountability and to snipe back at you while appearing to give "helpful" feedback. Decline the invitation to be blamed for something you did not do. Don't get stuck in the unproductive past. Refocus the discussion on the issue that currently separates you.

In dealing with Manipulators, you will find some of the tactics outlined in the chapters on Whiners and Wafflers useful. All of these players are characterized by passive-aggressive behaviour. Be mindful that Manipulators are neither Whiners nor Wafflers; they only use these tactics when it suits their purpose.

Manipulators are resentful people who fear not getting their fair share. Their distrust of others prompts them to use dirty tricks and change the rules in the middle of the game. Your counterstrategy must be to lock them into fair process and appropriate standards before the game begins. When their strategy is exposed, it loses its power.

17 MYOPICS

Some games are unintentional.

We all know we have some effect on the people around us. What we can never know with certainty is exactly how and to what extent we affect others. Consequently, there are a great many people who, despite our perceptions, are not being deliberately difficult. Nonetheless, they do give us a hard time and their behaviour does frustrate and demoralize us. Unfortunately, for us, they don't know this is happening. It's as if they are "short-sighted" when it comes to understanding how they negatively affect us. If they knew they were being difficult, with a little help, they would likely change their ways.

The challenge in dealing with Myopics is ours. We just haven't figured out how to communicate our concerns and annoyance to these people without making the situation worse. The reasons are many. Some of us are too polite, too considerate, too unassertive or we just can't be bothered. Most of us, however, lack the aptitude needed to broach the topic in a manner that will make a difference. We hope someone else will do the dirty deed for us. This rarely happens.

A few people blame their unassertiveness as contributing to the problem: "If only I could stand up to him and let him know what I really think, maybe he'd understand." Others try subtlety: "Maybe she'll get the hint." But no one will "get it" without having some appreciation of the specific nature of the problem. At the other end of the spectrum are those who take the bull by the horns and, in a condescending and patronizing tone, or in a fit of anger, tell the other player just how upsetting, disgusting or maddening his behaviour really is. Not surprisingly, this too doesn't work.

YOU NEVER TOLD ME

Susan was a child of the sixties. She had learned that good emotional health depended on personal acceptance and the open expression of feelings. She believed all her feelings (including anger, jealousy and sadness) were legitimate. Her friends described her as a "wonderful people person"—affectionate, sincere and caring. Her parents saw her as intelligent but moody and quick-tempered. Her first husband had viewed her as "a time bomb." He had complaints about Susan but by far the worst, as he saw it, was her tendency to "go off the deep end" at seemingly minor provocations.

Susan's current husband, Bill, would concur. When he first witnessed one of

Susan's explosions, he was shocked by the physical outburst. Besides yelling, screaming and flailing at him, she once threw a clock radio at his head. It missed, but barely. Bill's response? He was rational and calm. This was his normal reaction to an emotionally-charged situation. In a quiet voice, he would say, "Susan, calm down. It's pointless to act this way. You sound like a child. When you can behave like an adult, then we can discuss this problem." And Susan's reaction? Bill's patronizing, low-key and unsympathetic response only fuelled her rage. She stormed out, slamming the front door so hard that the glass shattered.

After an explosion, Susan would calm down quickly. In her mind, she had dealt with her anger appropriately. She had vented it. The explosion (her anger and the "fight" with Bill) were quickly forgotten. But Bill was left feeling angry and hurt. He thought she was emotionally immature. (Of course, Susan felt he was far too rational and uptight about his feelings. She believed that, if Bill really loved her, he should be able to accept her anger for what it was—a simple release of emotion.) The aftermath of these encounters could last several days with neither willing to apologize or, in some instances, even talk to each other.

As time passed, Susan's explosions occurred with less frequency and intensity. She stopped throwing things at Bill and he stopped taking her outbursts personally. As a result, they could usually resume a "normal" relationship a few hours after her explosions, rather than a couple of days.

Susan and Bill became parents. Little Mary was soon followed by Billy Jr. One day Susan saw the reaction of her children (then one and two years old) to her rage: "I was doing my usual ranting and raving. The kids were in no danger. I just needed to yell. I was in the middle of my tantrum when, all of a sudden, I saw their faces. Not only were they shocked and upset, they were SCARED. Scared of me, their own mother! The little guy actually began to sob. I was devastated. I never meant to scare my children. In fact, I never meant to scare anyone with my anger."

Susan's explosive behaviour had been difficult for her family. But they had been unable to communicate their concerns effectively. It was her children's frightened reaction that told her she had to change. She now knew the negative impact it was having on others. Susan suffered from behaviour myopia. Although she was aware her outbursts made her feel better, she could not see their effect on others. She never intended for her behaviour to cause fear, confusion and hurt in her loved ones.

The essence of communicating effectively with a Myopic is to find a non-threatening way to deliver your message, to do so in a manner that he'll actually hear what you're trying to say. This requires tact and creativity. Consider how Susan reacted when Bill tried to tell her about her behaviour. His words, his tone of voice and his rational approach only made the situation worse. As a result, she never really *heard* what he was trying to tell her. She reacted defensively to what she perceived as his lack of understanding and, worse, his judgmental put-down. Her children did, however, convey the message. They did it in a way that Susan could hear, loud and painfully clear. Not with words but with a look of terror on their faces.

THEY SIMPLY DON'T KNOW

Playing the game with a Myopic (getting him to appreciate your feelings of concern or frustration without making him feel defensive) requires planning and good confrontation skills. When you know how to confront this unintentional but challenging behaviour, you will discover that Myopics usually desire to change their ways. It's just that no one has told them before—that is, told them in a way that didn't make them feel defensive about their behaviour.

Myopics are unaware of the actual effects of their behaviour on others. They don't necessarily want to offend, frustrate or hurt you, as do many of the other players. So, when they do come to understand how their behaviour negatively affects you, they are generally amenable to changing their ways. Here's how to play this game.

First, consider your timing. Don't raise the sensitive issue of how they behave in an off-hand, innocuous or untimely manner. "Oh, by the way..." is not how to introduce the topic. Nor is it wise to begin the conversation when she is about to leave the office after a long hard day. There should be no other items on the agenda but how you feel about her behaviour. There should also be no distractions or interruptions, like a blaring stereo or a favourite TV program.

An advisable approach is to lead in tentatively by suggesting an appointment: "I'd like to talk with you about something that's been on my mind, Gavin. When would be a good time?" Leave yourself ample time for this meeting. While it could end quickly, it may also run on for some time. So don't pressure yourself with deadlines. If you are prepared to introduce this sensitive and possibly upsetting issue, you must be prepared to "hang in" until your objective is accomplished. Use the appointment method with family members as well. The kids will be intrigued. They'll feel important and you can be sure you'll have their full attention. Indeed, in the interim they may be wondering just what it is that you want to discuss. Focusing their attention on the issue is not a bad thing either.

If your Myopic asks about the nature of the meeting, you can be vague at this juncture: "It concerns a business matter," or "It's a personal matter" will suffice. If you give him too much information, he will spend the pre-appointment time imagining the worst and preparing his defence. Before you even open your mouth, he probably will have stopped listening.

So far so good. You've agreed to get together and you've allowed sufficient time to deal with the matter at hand. You may find yourself feeling nervous and anxious. "How do I begin the conversation? I don't want to offend him. Worse, I don't want him to take it the wrong way and jump down my throat. Maybe I shouldn't have made the appointment in the first place. Why me? Why can't someone else tell him what a miserable, rotten person he is?" Relax. You're psyching yourself out, not up. There's a method here and it does work. Planning and practice will ensure your success.

Begin the conversation by openly expressing your ambivalent feelings about the encounter. Tell him the truth, that you're not especially relishing this moment. People become defensive and resistant to criticism when they perceive the other person to be lecturing, preaching and moralizing. Instead, consider how the following lead into the discussion might be received: "You know this really isn't easy for me, Gavin. I don't want to upset you. But, this has been bothering me for awhile and I feel, if we don't discuss it, things may just go from bad to worse."

Do you think he's likely to jump down your throat with that introduction? I doubt it. You're neither attacking nor accusing. If anything, he's probably curious about the problem. Remember, he's the Myopic. He doesn't see that his behaviour is causing you a problem. And his perception that you're having an awkward time expressing your feelings will lead him to be more understanding of your plight, perhaps even to offer you some encouragement. "Take it easy, Bob. What's on your mind?" Reflect on your accomplishment (so far). You now have his attention and he is clearly less defensive than you expected. He seems prepared to listen. (Consider also that, if you are a boss or parent, your subordinate or child may never have heard you express your feelings so candidly. Your perceived vulnerability will lower their defences.)

There is another benefit to this opening. Acknowledging your own internal discomfort openly will lessen your anxiety. Saying how you feel about something frequently legitimizes what you have to say. You become a better player, less focused on your emotions and more aware of what needs to be said and how to say it.

The next step is the critical one. It's where most of us get derailed in spite of our good intentions. *Don't judge their behaviour.* When you tell people what they "should" or "should not" do, they become resistant. They don't hear you. They "get their backs up" and either respond with defensiveness or, worse, counter with an accusation. Remember your primary objective is to find a way to be heard.

WORDS TO AVOID

Despite your good intentions, some words and phrases will only inflame the situation. Take *always* and *never*, for example. When you direct these judgmental words at another player, you're guaranteed a defensive reaction. For example, when you say "Helen, you never make your bed when I ask you," her instinctive response is to counter, "That's not true. I made it last week, on Monday to be exact." Normal, self-respecting people do two things when under attack. First, they protect themselves from the perceived threat. Second, they counterattack. "You're *always* on my back. Give me a break!" That's a good way to start an unnecessary conflict. Use judgmental words or tones and you'll be in the midst of a negative interaction cycle before you know it.

Here's another situation. What would you say to a colleague who never has a good word to say about anybody or anything? A chronic Whiner. What you might like to say is: "Dan, I'm sick of your constant criticism. I also think you are an incredible bore...and a stupid one at that." Feel better? Probably. But have you changed his behaviour? Have you played the game or just blurted out an unthinking, emotional response? He certainly didn't get your real message and now he sees you as both unfair and rude—two more things he can add to his list when he complains about you to others.

So what do you say? Make it *personal*. Rather than judging his behaviour, tell him as specifically and honestly as possible how it affects you. Replace the accusing, attacking and aggressive "you" in your description of the offending behaviour with an "I": "When I hear destructive criticism, I get irritated and I stop listening. I really don't hear what you're trying to tell me. And I'm sure that's not what you want."

See the difference? A better choice of words produces a better result. Now he knows exactly how his behaviour affects you. He can weigh the consequences of his behaviour objectively since he doesn't feel judged or attacked. Is that how he really wants you to feel? Is his criticism accomplishing what it is intended to do? Probably not.

Consider your phrasing carefully. Suppose you had said: "Dan, when you criticize me all the time, I just get irritated and stop listening." Not as effective, is it? The problem is the trigger phrase, "all the time." Put yourself in Dan's shoes. He might respond with something like: "I don't criticize you *all the time*. Why, just yesterday, I complimented you on the Anderson proposal. Didn't I?"

In a conflict situation, how you say something is more important that what you say. I have seen people struggle repeatedly with the phrasing of their tactics. Their biggest complaint is: "But that's not the sort of thing that I would say in that situation." True. That's why they usually lose the game. What you normally say in most encounters, especially those that are charged with tension, is an unrehearsed, unthinking emotional response. You are acting from habit, doing what feels most comfortable. And it typically backfires. Don't let your ego get in the way of your objectives. Learn how to play the game. If you aren't winning consistently, there must be a better way.

REHEARSE. REHEARSE. REHEARSE.

Rational *action* is always preferable to emotional reaction. The key is to have a game plan and to rehearse until you are comfortable with the phrasing. Your objective is clear: to be heard. With that in mind, preparation is invaluable. Not only will you begin to feel more comfortable with these more effective phrases, you are also better positioned to anticipate the Myopic's likely counters.

The best way to rehearse is with a partner, preferably someone who doesn't know the Myopic. (When you choose a partner who knows the other person, the tendency is to commiserate about your plight rather than finding creative new ways to deal with the problem.) Whether or not you have a rehearsal partner, it is helpful to write down what you plan to say. Study it, edit it and practise it until it fits you like a comfortable old shoe. It may seem like overkill for such a short encounter but practice is the foundation of success in any game. Now you are ready to try again.

"Dan, there are times when I'm at a loss for words when we talk. Like this morning for example. You came to me about the telephone problem. When I offered a suggestion for solving it, you ignored me and went on to criticize me for missing a deadline. Sometimes I get the feeling that you enjoy criticizing me. And that kills my enthusiasm for wanting to improve the situation. What are your thoughts on this?"

A much better execution of the plan. You have described the problem with non-judgmental words, "I" statements and specific examples. You haven't told him what he *should* do. Also, you are being collaborative—asking for his feedback. You could go a step further and give Dan some positive reinforcement. For example, "Dan, I like it so much better when we can collaborate on projects, like the new company newsletter. Or when you occasionally point out what I'm doing right, like your comment yesterday on the Anderson report." Dan now has an accurate idea of what behaviour you do like and what motivates you. He feels valued as well.

Finally, it's time to stop and listen. You've made your point. Don't weaken it by providing more details. Human beings are the only creatures who know how to talk themselves into trouble. While the hardest thing to do in a conflict situation is to shut up, it's the best thing you can do once you've made your point.

Chances are Dan will be surprised by your frank revelation. You've just given him some new information—perhaps something he hasn't heard before and certainly not from you and you've given it to him in a non-threatening, even supportive way. He might be upset by your comments and he may need some time to reflect on them. But that's okay. He might also ask you for more information for clarification: "Do you really think I *like* to criticize you? I mean how often do I criticize anyway? Do other people think that way?" Asking questions, *v.s.* defending one's behaviour, signifies that the Myopic is beginning to learn a better way.

When planning your encounter, try to anticipate all possible reactions the Myopic might have to your observations. Prepare an appropriate response for each. If you don't, he may easily draw you into your old, predictable patterns by pressing a hot button. And your unthinking response will lose the game. If Dan were to say, "Give me an example," you must oblige with something specific. If you say, "An example! I can't think of one. I could have thought of a hundred yesterday, but I can't think of any today", you've lost your credibility.

Dan is clearly in a learning mode, receptive to more information provided it's constructively offered. This is your opportunity to give him additional feedback about the problem and, in so doing, to collaborate on solutions to correcting the behaviour that impairs the working relationship. When you observe this learning mode, your typecasting of the behaviour is confirmed.

However, at this phase of the game, another reaction is possible. Dan may get defensive (despite your best efforts) and may seek to either explain or justify his actions. He might even attack you or your motives for raising the issue. "I know I criticize people. I have to. If I didn't, they'd never improve." This response tells you you're not dealing with a Myopic. It's another player whom you have yet to identify. A Bully? A Tough Guy? A Know-it-all perhaps? Your adversary is not a Myopic because he is obviously aware that his behaviour offends you. As such, he's not about to apologize, make excuses or change it for you...or anyone else. His response to your efforts so far is to reject your game plan by telling you that you're either "crazy" or "too damn sensitive" or by explaining why he does it.

You now have a choice to make. (As you're discovering, the game of life is all about making the right strategic choices.) You can terminate the discussion and go back to the drawing board to work up a plan for another game, once you properly label the player in your midst. Alternatively, you could give Dan the benefit of the doubt. You could chalk up this defensive outburst as merely consistent with his behaviour and carry on. It's called persistence. It's understanding the importance of process. The question you have to answer now is "*Is it worth the effort?*" After this cost-benefit analysis, you can decide whether you want to continue the game.

PERSISTENCE OFTEN PAYS

Part of your rehearsal should include anticipating negative reactions. Which is why, when you hear Dan reject the opportunity to learn more about his behaviour, you shouldn't be overly concerned. He's still with you and you're still communicating. Depending on what Dan is saying, you could do some active listening: nod, lean forward and grunt encouragingly. When he finally stops talking, be sure you've heard it all by asking "Anything else?" When there's nothing else, reflect back in your own words what Dan has told you until you're both satisfied that you understand what he's saying.

Once Dan has vented, you may find him more willing to listen to your opinion which you will now state (again) in a non-judgmental, calm and supportive tone. "Dan, I really value your thoughts on this. I want to hear more provided it's constructive and I can learn from it." Maybe he might now say, "But, if you were responsible, you'd want to know what your problems are." He's right, in a way. But, don't back down now. Keep focused on the objective. You're playing well.

"You're right, Dan. I am responsible and I do like to be on top of things. Let me give you a couple of specific examples of the kind of criticisms that aren't too helpful." Remain calm, be supportive, practise effective listening skills, stick to "I" messages and deal with specific behaviours. These tactics will keep the communication lines open and, eventually, you will be heard.

Be patient. It may take more time than you realize. But, usually with Myopics, it's easier than you think. Done well and without judgement or unnecessary embellishment, what you're saying really is news to them. A friend once told me he had tried this strategy with his boss, whom he had diagnosed as Myopic, and it failed. However, to his amazement, his boss called him a month later after a lengthy vacation to say, "You know, I've been thinking about what you told me awhile ago— you know, about my bullying people. And, I think you're right. I'd like to get some suggestions from you on how I can change some of that. Do you mind?"

Changing (or modifying) one's behaviour does take time. That's because, before it can occur, people need sufficient time to *hear* the concerns, to weigh the consequences and to get accustomed to the idea that such change can be beneficial in their significant relationships. People rarely understand the message the first time, especially if there is a lack of tact, creativity and diplomacy. The natural (human) tendency is to resist and reject such information. A good player understands his adversary and persists with the game plan, looking for signals and opportunities to make progress. He also knows he may have to play the game again to reinforce the desired behaviour.

Just because the Myopic has heard you and appears willing to act on your observations and suggestions, don't assume the game is over. People often tell me, "I tried your idea and it worked! For about two weeks. Then she slipped back to her old ways and here I am again, frustrated and fed up." That's understandable. Were it otherwise, it wouldn't be called the game of life.

Old habits are hard to break, even when we really want to change them. Witness your overweight friends who keep trying one diet after another or colleagues attempting to quit smoking. They want to change but they haven't discovered that they need to replace the bad habit with a more productive one. Every time the desired behaviour occurs, you need to say something positive. And be specific: "Dan, I really appreciated your encouragement this morning at the staff meeting."

Should you find there is nothing to be positive about, that there have been no changes since your first talk, then it may be time to go back to the playing field again. Perhaps you weren't specific enough. Persistence, process and good tactics will always win out. Keep focused on problem solving. Myopics, in particular, are as anxious as are you to change the offensive behaviour. "Dan, are there some things we can do to improve this situation? Any ideas?" Add your own ideas to the list after Dan has given his, get a commitment on one or two strategies and then agree to follow up in a more structured way.

Behavioural change requires positive reinforcement, frequently and liberally. In this game, you cannot be a spectator.

18 NO PEOPLE

Patience is the antidote to negativism.

The No People are negativists. They are people who have little faith in either themselves or the future. Obstructionists to almost every novel scheme or idea, they normally respond to productive suggestions and interesting concepts with such killer phrases as: "We tried that last year. They'll never let us do it." They are stubborn just for the sake of being stubborn.

Truly classic naysayers suffer from a victim mentality. Simply put, this is an attitude that says: "My life is essentially at the mercy of vast, powerful forces beyond my control. Accordingly, I am the victim of my upbringing, my genes, my social class, my education, my parents, my teachers, my spouse, my boss, the economy, the times we live in, politicians, large corporations, the rich." The list can go on without end.

If you suffer from this debilitating outlook, it really makes little difference what you want out of life. Since you are relatively powerless, you must learn to settle for whatever life gives you. Right? Rarely will you go out of your way to seek more than what is offered. The victim mentality ultimately discharges you from any real responsibility for your life, since clearly what befalls you is not your fault. The number of people inflicted with this counterproductive outlook on life, albeit to different degrees, is greater than you might imagine. In some social and occupational groups, the infliction is epidemic.

Sometimes, of course, we actually are at the mercy of forces over which we have little or no control—a hurricane, an earthquake or even the uncertainty of change. But, there is a vast difference between being a victim (which we all can become in some areas of our lives) and having the victim mentality.

A victim mentality robs you of any interest in constructive suggestions or new ideas. After all, what's the use of thinking about them, much less trying to implement them? It's such work and the results are so uncertain. Why even bother? Perhaps you've heard this familiar lament: *The things you suggest may help other people, but they can't offer any hope to me.*

PUTTING PESSIMISTS IN PLACE

Pessimism is often contagious. Many adults prefer to dwell on the worst possible scenario. It's our nature. We've learned that it is better to be safe than sorry. So, to influence a negativist, you need incredible patience, optimism and concentration.

It's critical that you stay focused on your own realistic optimism when No People present you with a litany of reasons why your proposals "just won't work". You have to illustrate your points with conviction and reinforce them with examples of previous successes. Cite viable choices, opportunities and alternatives. Suggest that previous failures need not get in the way of future successes. And the ultimate test of your own optimism may well be the decision, when necessary, to go it alone.

Never argue with No People. They rarely admit they're wrong. You can't win an argument with a naysayer. Rather, describe your alternatives and ideas without implying a judgment on their possible success or failure. Phrase your recommendations as proposals for assessment. *"What do you think would happen if we...?"* is a tactful way of introducing your thoughts and recommendations, however conclusive they might be. Plan for the obvious response. Anticipate that their counters will be negative. Stay focused on your primary objective, which is to get them at least to "consider" your ideas. Don't rush into proposing your best alternative or solution right at the outset of the discussion, because No People enjoy shooting down good ideas. And they do it so well.

Very few people, including negativists, would want to appear to be closed-minded, rigid and inflexible even though they probably are. So try to use appropriate and tactful phrasing. Since your objective is to get them to fairly evaluate or consider your proposal, observe what happens when you use that exact wording: "Would you at least *consider* it by hearing me out?"

Since you know the pessimist's first response to your suggestions probably will be negative, prepare for it. Don't be put off by his killer phrases. The No People need time to come around. Their opposition is an habitual reaction to even the most brilliant idea or proposal. *Patience is the antidote to negativism.*

Pessimists have the ability to defeat even the most brilliant ideas simply by implying that the worst possible scenario will likely ensue. That is probably the Achilles' heel of any rational person or group. The best defence is to make these naysayers accountable for their depiction of dire circumstances. Agree with their portrayal of the worst imaginable consequence and then ask, *"Well, what would probably happen then?"* Forget about trying to reason with their negative assumptions. Agree with them. Then ask what we'll do about it when the sky falls. This useful question will help them separate their real fear from an impossible fantasy. Moreover, it tends to get them focused on possible solutions should that dreaded prediction come to pass.

Most pessimists are just looking for a good argument. Call them on it and observe what happens: *"I get the impression that no matter what I say, you're not going to agree."* When confronted in such a forthright manner, the average negativist will tone down his opposition to your ideas. You'll also start to appreciate how their game works.

Here are a few further thoughts on how to deal with people who seem to oppose just about everything you say. If you can, get the naysayer to think that your idea was really his, perhaps by subtly criticizing a constructive idea just enough to make him attempt to defend it. Also, try to let the negativist express himself first and permit or encourage him to expound on his thoughts (if he is so inclined). This is a useful form of venting. If the opposition is to come, why not get it out of the way up front? In general, people accept suggestions more quickly when first given the opportunity to state their objections, in which case their subsequent counter-arguments become a bit like spent ammunition. While we might all like to hear others agree with our viewpoints, failing that, we at least want our views acknowledged.

When you must give instructions to subordinates who are frequently negative or otherwise opposed to your directives, try phrasing them as requests. If necessary, you can always use your authority. The important thing is to be consistent and to stress the necessity of achieving common (corporate or relationship) goals. Make a special effort to focus on "we" ideas rather than focusing on adversarial positions. When initiating a new procedure, keep in mind that employees with chronic negative attitudes are not reliable indicators of either the viability or the success of your ideas. No People rarely work well with others. So don't kid yourself. Plan for the impact naysayers typically have on organizational life. Then prepare your game plan.

As always, remember the importance of perspective. Some people do have legitimate complaints and reasons for opposing seemingly constructive suggestions. There is usually a shred of substance in a negativist's accusations and discontent. Pessimism can occasionally be a valuable counterweight to unbridled optimism.

THE MEANING OF NO

In dealing with negativists, it's important to understand the meaning and consequences of "no." Clearly, the word means different things to different people. To a negotiator, it's merely a position in time. To a child, it's an open invitation to challenge parental authority. To the conflict manager, it's firm confrontation. To an unquestioning subordinate, it's rejection carved in stone. To a literalist, it's lost opportunity. To a pessimist, it's a way of life.

Depending upon its timing, phrasing and non-verbal support, the speaker and the context, "no" has a multitude of possible meanings: I'm not sure; I don't understand; I need more information; it's the wrong time; or, perhaps, I need more time.

"No" is often a tactic, used consciously as well as unconsciously, to lower expectations or to misdirect. It might signify an objection to a part of your argument rather than the whole. Indeed, in a negotiation, objections are neither interruptions nor rejections but an integral part of the process. Curiously, objections can indicate a genuine interest in the proposals under discussion and thus should be viewed as an effort to understand or clarify.

The first time a naysayer raises an objection, you should try to ignore it. People don't seek agreement to their every reservation (to assume the contrary would be naive). In the absence of support or resistance, most objections typically evaporate. Should they persist, and should you wish to advance your position, follow the salesman's dictum: If they object to the price, talk about quality; if they object to quality, talk about service; if they object to service, talk about terms.

In playing the game with the No People, listen to the actual words they use and observe the non-verbal support. Often the phrasing or subsequent rationale will reveal a lack of firmness or indicate some room to manoeuvre. Resist the natural tendency to react emotionally, get tough or withdraw. "No" is an emotional trigger. Remind yourself that differences of opinion are normal and that "no" is neither absolute nor personal, unless you make it so.

If you must deal with negativists, learn to negotiate with them. Seek a compromise if necessary. Trade off the present for the uncertain future. Propose an alternative that would still satisfy your essential needs or minimum objectives. Use the "I cut, you choose" method: one person decides the division, the other has first choice as to which portion he will take. Try deciding the issue by reference to an acceptable objective measure, like marketplace value or professional standards. Finally, if creative negotiating strategies fail, have a neutral third party decide the issue or flip a coin. The latter approach is not a cop-out; it can be a face-saving way to resolve the issue when the difference is insignificant or has become personal.

GUIDELINES FOR NO

There will be times in the game when you too must negate the ideas and proposals of others. If you don't want to be perceived as one of the No People in doing so, here are a few guidelines for saying "no."

It is appropriate to say "no" whenever the other player makes thoughtless or inappropriate remarks; when you're asked to do something he should be doing for himself; when committing others against their will; when you can't deliver on what is asked; when you are given an unreasonable deadline; and when saying "yes" would obligate you to unacceptable commitments later. Say "no" to requests which conflict with your priorities, or to small, nibbling side conditions after a basic agreement has been reached.

The way you say "no" is critical to making it stick. "No" is at its most powerful when unexplained. The more you seek to justify your "no", the less likely people will believe it. Shakespeare said it best: "Methinks she doth protest too much." Give reasons in support of your objection and people will attack the reasons and thus undermine the "no".

Say "no" promptly but not impatiently or in anger. A soft "no" is hard to rebut. Reject the proposal without rejecting the proposer. Demonstrate that you heard what he said by restating his viewpoint. "I know it is a worthy cause and I do value our friendship. But my answer is no."

The key to playing the game with pessimists is threefold: be creative, use tact and be persistent.

19 OYSTERS

A stare of expectancy speaks volumes.

Oysters are silent, non-responsive types. They are generally passive people who tend to "clam up", especially in the presence of aggressive types or when confronted with conflict. While their silence typically results from shyness or attempts to evade difficult situations, it can also be used as a form of calculated aggression. Indeed, their silence is often situationally motivated.

Oysters have a behavioural tendency to react to probes into their privacy, or to any disagreeable situation for that matter, by closing down. Almost every question, no matter how harmless or innocuous, is perceived as an invasion of their personal space. They either won't or can't respond. It's as if they go out of their way to avoid answering direct questions.

An Oyster's success in being unresponsive is reinforced by those who don't know how to crack open their shell, the silence barrier. We are invariably defeated, not so much by their strategy of defence but by our own frustration and impatience. We let them off the hook either by talking, asking even more pointed questions, openly displaying our exasperation, answering for them or simply giving up. These responses signal victory to the oyster. It is we who help them evade the need to respond.

These silent ones are typecast as Oysters for an obvious reason. When you know how to open them up expertly, without damaging their fragile egos, you're likely to discover a few pearls—not the least of which is the kind of communication that can lead to a better, more productive relationship. The secret of course is knowing how to wait them out or, in some cases, draw them out of their shells.

OPENING THE SHELL

The first rule in playing the game with Oysters is not to let them escape. They have learned over time that the odds are great you will either do all the talking or, better still, eventually go away. Every time you fulfill that expectation, you've unintentionally rewarded and thus reinforced this annoying behaviour. These people are most likely to respond to your pleading enquiry "Don't you have *anything* to say about this?" with a meek and submissive "Can I go now?"

Your principle objective is straightforward: get them to talk. Their silence is creating stress for you, not them. Difficult as it may seem, you must resist that natural urge to break the tension by opening up first. But waiting them out without stress or anxiety requires a plan of action and some special tactics. Here they are.

Always use open-ended questions. Don't ask *"Do you like this?"* Rather, asking *"How do you feel about this?"* is more effective. Instead of getting one of only two possible responses (yes or no), both of which will freeze the conversation where it stands—in your hands—an open-ended question creates the potential for receiving more information with which to continue the discussion.

When you're confronted with a blank stare in response to your query, discover the benefits of communicating without talking. Remember that all of you is communicating. Use non-verbal gestures to put the pressure on them, not you. A silent stare of expectancy (conveying the expectation that they are about to answer your question) can speak volumes. Holding your open hand out to them also conveys a powerful *"give me something...fill it"* message. Since you are communicating, albeit not by talking, you've relieved your tension while increasing theirs.

Learn the importance of commenting on what's not happening: *"You're not giving me your thoughts on this, Pat."* Once again, you're communicating but not letting him off the hook. Alternatively, you might comment on his distress, as in *"I can see you're having a problem with this, Mark."* Always await his response with supportive non-verbal gestures. Should you want to ease the tension somewhat, you might try a less direct side-bar question—something like *"Have you seen Scott today?"* This non-threatening query will permit him to open up without dealing with your main concern.

Prying open Oysters takes time. Their best defence is your own impatience. Counter this manoeuvre by setting yourself a time limit. Give yourself twenty minutes to achieve your goal. Most of us, of course, would give up within the first five minutes or less. But if you know you're going to be there for twenty minutes, and if you use tact and creativity, you're less likely to feel pressure or frustration. After ten minutes, a quick glance at your watch will remind you that you've still got another ten to go.

EFFECTIVE COUNTERS

Since you've been in this situation before, you can anticipate their favourite responses: *"Nothing"* or *"I don't know."* The best counters to such annoying replies are non-directive responses (also known as eloquent grunting, as in *"uh huh"*), supportive non-verbal signals (like a look of concern) or prompts for more information (*"What else?"* or *"Anything more?"*). These kinds of questions keep the pressure on them while relieving your anxiety about the silence.

Another useful comeback to the frustrating "I don't know" response, especially in dealing with uncooperative children, is to say, "*If you could know, what might that be?*" This wishful, almost playful query might intrigue them. It's not quite the reply they expect. The point, of course, is to use creativity to keep the pressure on without escalating the confrontation by raising your voice. Don't defeat yourself. Nothing will make an Oyster clam up more quickly than the perception of an open conflict.

What happens when they do, finally, open up? Prepare yourself. The game is not over. When they do talk, it's likely that they won't want to discuss your agenda items. They will be oblique. Don't interject with "*That's not what we're talking about, Jessica!*" If you do, you'll find yourself right back at square one. The primary objective is to get them to talk, not necessarily to talk specifically about your concerns. That's objective number two.

Your purpose is to assure them that a conversation with you is not a threatening experience and that their typical silence and unresponsiveness just doesn't work on you. So, when they finally open up, let them be oblique. Remember the game is about making progress, not achieving perfection.

Should your best efforts fail, all is not lost. The third ingredient in winning this game is persistence. Remind them that it's not over. You will want to meet again to discuss this issue. Make another appointment and set aside sufficient time for round two.

Perhaps you'd like to set a trap to snare the ever evasive Oyster. Try this one. End the meeting with "I can see that you want to give this some more thought, Eric. Why don't you take some time and put your ideas in writing. Send me a memo on it."

When Eric's memo arrives, you can now call the next meeting. This time, however, begin the encounter with something like this: "There are a few things in your note that I don't quite understand, Eric. I wonder if you could help me by explaining the third paragraph in particular. Here, I've underlined the section that I would like you to expand upon." Works like a charm. And consider the reward that may await. Nice shiny pearls. (This tactic also works well with children. Often, Oysters are better able to articulate their feelings in writing.)

The key to this game, as with most, is to be patient and focused. Set limited objectives and advance your cause. Forget the home runs; you're more likely to strike out trying. Keep hitting singles and you'll win this game.

20 TOUGH GUYS

Be honest and direct.

Tough Guys are rebels who have decided that the price of attempting to please others is simply too high. Their purpose in life is to prove that they can get by without anyone's help, that they can make it through difficult situations quite nicely on their own. It's almost as if they really haven't progressed much from their belligerent early teen years.

Tough Guys have an aversion to dependence and accommodation. They refuse to justify their behaviour since they perceive themselves as accountable to no one. They don't want to be committed, tied down to anyone or anything. Not surprisingly, they are distrustful of authority figures and they rail against procedural limits and policy of any kind. They resent being defined by what they do. Rather, they like to be known for what they can accomplish. As a result, Tough Guys are independent and highly productive people.

A Tough Guy can be a workaholic building a career against all odds or the driving professional woman seeking a top management position in a male-dominated corporation. As with all challenging players, you encounter Tough Guys in every walk of life. But you are more likely to discover them in the business world, where competition is the norm.

Tough Guys have a need to prove themselves, to be self-sufficient, able and respected. They are typically impatient loners, determined to reach the top and easily angered by those whom they view as obstacles to their goals (although their main competitors are rarely others and often themselves). Their power resides in their mental toughness, self-reliance and sheer productive output.

That's what makes them such tough bosses. Their normal response to under-production or failure is a terse "I don't want excuses. I want results!" But they are also logical, goal-oriented and effective problem solvers. They analyse their subordinates' ideas and suggestions for their practical implications and bottom-line impact.

Tough Guys tend to be black-and-white thinkers, viewing people, problems and events in terms of extremes. They use this tactic to move others away from their positions. They focus on differences in positions rather than on similarities as a means of generating conflict. Hence, they disagree a lot—the object being to challenge and, in the process, demonstrate their superior grasp of the issues. They prefer to beat people rather than try to understand them.

They are disciplined, focused, aloof and incisive people, likely to be more impressed by hard evidence than by concepts, theories, or advice from authorities. Tough Guys are "show me" people and this attitude is usually communicated to others as "put up or shut up!" They believe that if you want something done right, you've got to do it yourself. And they do: "I'll do it...but on my terms."

Not surprisingly, Tough Guys are difficult to get along with. They counter rules, tradition, established patterns and authorities with sarcasm, arrogance and civil disobedience. "Just tell me what you want done. I'll figure it out for myself and I'll do it my way."

FINDING THE SOFT SPOT

Like every player in the game of life, Tough Guys have needs. Once you understand them and can align yourself with those "soft spots," you can influence their behaviour. Curiously, Tough Guys are inwardly afraid that they just might not make it. Part of their desire to explore and create—a positive attribute—is a need to experiment with who they might like to be.

Tough Guys sense that if they are not rebellious and tough at all times, they might become dependent on others. They have a tendency to overstate their self-confidence in order to protect themselves. Acting tough keeps others off balance. Hence, their tactics are designed to keep others at a distance. What follows are some useful countertactics and thoughts on how to play their game.

When Tough Guys challenge your traditional ways, your authority, or your credentials, don't fight back. Their purpose is to take the offensive by placing the burden of proof and justification on you. It's a highly effective tactic, because (as noted) we frequently talk ourselves into trouble. Don't get sucked in. Don't give them the chance to undermine or discredit your position or your confidence. Rather than getting defensive, tell them what you agree with, then ask them to explain their reasons for challenging you. Ask them why your explanation would be important to them. Probe the underlying issues rather than providing ammunition for energizing your differences. Above all, resist the urge to justify your own position.

Here's some useful language to use whenever a Tough Guy rebels against the established way of doing things (assuming, that is, you agree with that established procedure). "I agree that the old way may not necessarily be the best way of doing this. And continuing to do something just because we've always done it that way doesn't really make a lot of sense. Tell me more about your ideas and let's see if we can't incorporate them into our normal routines. We might find the best of both worlds." Indeed, you just might. More importantly, you're turning a potential conflict into an opportunity for cooperation.

Sometimes our efforts at confronting a Tough Guy's perceived "holier than thou" attitude only evokes our own sense of self-righteousness. This is of course counterproductive. A better response is to describe their behaviour, let them know in specific terms how it affects you and invite them not to treat you with such disdain. (It's important to remember that these people are not like Bullies, who are mean-spirited and really do want to hurt you.) With Tough Guys, you can be honest, simple and direct. It's effective because they really are tough. They can take it without having to hit back.

Here's how to do it. "Your remarks make me feel like an idiot, Ryan. And I don't especially like being put down like that. Can't we try to engage one another on equal terms, with respect for each other's views, instead of having to win all the time?" If you don't feel up to a direct challenge, try asking an honest question. "Am I doing something to you that makes you want to treat me as an inferior?"

Don't allow yourself to be intimidated. Unlike Bullies, Tough Guys have a bark that is much worse than their bite. Confront their behaviour and encourage them to be more constructive by focusing on the real issues. "I don't wish to be treated like a child, Nancy. And I don't find your sarcasm amusing. I do want to resolve our problem and find a solution that is mutually acceptable. Let's focus on the real issue and work this out. Are you willing to cooperate with me on this?"

Avoid becoming the critical parent in the face of their rebellious behaviour. Explain that you want only to understand them, not fight with them. "I'm not asking you to justify your behaviour. I just want to understand it, if I can." Stress the mutual benefits of understanding each other's needs and motives better. Explain why you want to know: "I end up feeling as if I can't really trust you when you won't tell me why you did that." We all relate better to consequences and benefits than to threats and demands. Even Tough Guys.

You can be honest with Tough Guys. Point out that your problem is how they behave or lead others to feel inadequate, not their view of authority or procedures. Hold them accountable and describe clearly the consequences of their actions or non-actions. Outline the benefits of cooperation in working through the problem. Encourage creativity; it's usually one of their strong suits. "I'm not suggesting we ignore the policies around here. I am asking you to deal honestly with this problem and to work with me in finding a creative way of resolving it."

The best way to play the game with Tough Guys is not to "out-tough" them. Get them to work with you by demonstrating creative and positive outcomes. Don't make it a test of wills or one-upmanship. Keep focused on convergent interests and resist the temptation to discuss your differences. Use warmth and humour: "You look as though you could be a lot of fun if you weren't such a tough guy."

As always, do your homework. Keep it clean and simple. And don't take Tough Guys too seriously. Their challenging of authority is what progress is all about.

21 WAFFLERS

Make it easy for them.

There is no greater frustration for highly motivated and creative subordinates than toiling in the debilitating shadow of an indecisive boss. Vacillators in subordinate positions are less troublesome because, when necessary, you can make the decision for them.

Wafflers are people who prolong the decision-making process or, worse, endeavour to avoid it, to absurd and unproductive limits. The main challenge for those who have the misfortune to be plagued by such procrastinators is that they are normally pleasant and outwardly supportive people. They appear genuinely motivated to be helpful. Therein lies our frustration. Wafflers can't or won't say "no" because they fear the loss of our approval. This creates a terrible dilemma for them, especially when they have no choice but to make decisions.

Wafflers have a basic need to want to please everyone. They can't make decisions because they can't bear to hurt anyone. They believe the "right" decision is the one that benefits everyone. Thus, they seek to do things in a manner that will contribute most to everybody's welfare. Like Charlie Brown, indecisives assume that the need to make difficult decisions usually disappears over time.

Rarely is their well-meaning intention in the best interest of either the relationship or the organization. In a competitive marketplace and in today's workplace, where resources are finite, tough decisions are required. But Wafflers can't seem to divide up the pie when it's necessary; they want a pie for everyone.

So how do you play the game with Wafflers? Whether he is your boss, colleague or spouse, here are a few tactics aimed at influencing indecisive people.

REASSURE THEM

These players need constant reassurance. They need to hear that you won't be offended or wounded by their objections or their reservations to your ideas and proposals. You may tire of the necessity to give such strokes but, as you've discovered, persistence is an essential ingredient in the games you choose to play. Help them to be candid with you by providing clear evidence of your support. Point out that others who might be affected would probably agree with their decision. Then add your own reinforcement, "In my view, Mark, you've done the *right* thing."

When dealing with subordinates, your purpose should be to seek commitment rather than compliance. Incremental gains will prove superior to quantum leaps when attempting to modify the behaviour of a procrastinator. Don't threaten to punish an employee for missing a promised deadline. It's more productive to give him a role in scheduling the project. Giving indecisives a stake in the process of decision making is essential to increasing their comfort with that process.

In the same vein, you should focus the vacillator's attention on getting started with a task rather than on finishing it. Your efforts will be more fruitful and less distressing by keeping them moving, however slowly, towards easily reachable interim objectives. Wafflers are unduly stressed and often incapacitated when asked to focus on a distant goal.

Progress is more likely with indecisive subordinates when you use praise and encouragement rather than anger or criticism. An angry rebuke to a missed deadline usually results in further procrastination. Build on strength even if you must resort to searching for the opportunities to praise.

BUREAUCRATS AT HEART

If you're dealing with a boss who has an overriding need to have her decisions accepted by everyone in the organization before she'll make them, discuss the idea with your peers before bringing it forward for approval. If the boss reacts to your request or recommendation with, "The others won't like it, I'm sure," an appropriate counter is to point out that you have already consulted with them and obtained their support of the change you're proposing.

Better still, find something in the company policy manual that supports what you want to do, at least in principle. Wafflers, after all, are bureaucrats at heart. They like to go by "the book." Use company jargon or terms that will appeal to those who are above your boss. Try to relate your idea to the organization's key goals, values or mission.

Seek to determine the real reasons for their indecisiveness. You'll likely have to do a bit of probing to discover this information before you attempt to problem solve with them. Keep in mind, however, that Wafflers are masters of indirect communication. They prefer evasive and justifying responses to your direct probes. They rarely tell outright lies; they just don't tell the whole truth. Listen to their exact words and question the double-talk. What does, "All in all, your report is *generally* okay" really mean? Or how about this favourite: "There's no doubt in my mind that that's what we *should* do." But will she do it? You'll never know unless you ask.

Focus your efforts on identifying any underlying, sensitive issues that might be impeding his decision making but do so in a non-threatening way. Try to isolate and define the essence of the difficulty while seeking to understand his internal conflict. Keep in mind too that you or your style may be one of the causes of his discomfort. If you suspect this is the case, ask specific questions designed to get the topic out in the open where you can both deal with it: "Am I being too pushy about this, Chris?"

Encourage problem solving. Generate alternatives without judgment. But remember also that too many alternatives will overwhelm the Waffler and reinforce his propensity for indecision.

Support your proposals and ideas with hard evidence. Endeavour to provide three reasons why your idea should be accepted. Two may not be enough and four may be too many. Recommend a course of action by reference to impartial standards, objective criteria or even motherhood statements (things like quality, service, fair and reasonable, professional standards, business ethics and the like). Wafflers rarely disagree with motherhood.

If all else fails, attempt to keep control of your proposals or projects in your own hands. Indeed, a concrete plan of action is essential. Changing priorities in the middle of a project will only induce greater indecision on the part of Wafflers. You will need the courage of your convictions in assuming direct responsibility for any possible risk. If necessary, trade in a trust credit: "Look boss, I'd like to run with this one. If it doesn't work out, I'll take the flak."

Try to take the risk of failure off the Waffler's shoulders. Should you be successful, you will probably have to share the glory. True; it's unfair. But don't allow your ego to get in the way of your objectives. Your purpose is to get these people comfortable with the thought of making decisions so that your life and your relationship will become more productive.

Finally, watch for signs of emotional overload. Indecisives stress easily. If pushed too hard, they are prone to make impulsive and thus often bad decisions. Observe the telltale non-verbal signs of stress overload—behavioural patterns that indicate that her stress tolerance threshold has been reached. Signals like a pronounced sucking of air or vigorously scratching the scalp would suggest the wisdom of leaving the issue for another day. Your objective in playing this game is to achieve incremental movement toward your goal. Quantum leaps may be risky and counterproductive.

As always, don't lose your perspective. Everyone is, or at least ought to be, indecisive at times. Sometimes Wafflers prefer not to move for valid reasons. Try to discover those reasons before using these tactics.

A PERFECT WAFFLER

The most important aspect of playing this game is understanding the cause of the behaviour. While Wafflers procrastinate because of their basic need to please others, they do so for different reasons.

Mavis is a classic procrastinator. She's bright, competent, well-educated and personable. She started at EDC Electronics 10 years ago as a secretary. Now she's the office manager. When she started, senior management felt she had the ability to move quickly into a supervisory role. But, as she was given more and more responsibility, something seemed to go wrong. She became unwilling or unable to follow through on tasks.

Although Mavis was as personable as ever and would accept jobs without hesitation, she didn't get around to completing them (or even starting some of them). The jobs she did finish were always done well. Her creativity and attention to detail ensured that virtually all her projects were flawless. In fact, she had never been known to turn in anything that was less than perfect. But she had also developed a reputation among her co-workers as "Maybe Mavis". The standing joke was "you may get it on time or you may not."

Not surprisingly, her colleagues had learned to give her plenty of time to complete projects. Indeed, her boss had learned the wisdom of giving Mavis a buffer period between the apparent deadline and when he actually needed the work done. But it was not as easy for Mavis' subordinates. Whenever they asked her for a decision (especially those involving performance appraisals or promotions), she cheerfully agreed to deal with the concern at her earliest possible opportunity. Unfortunately, her staff never heard about it again. It was difficult to criticize her since everyone agreed she was a great boss—pleasant, cheerful and well-respected. If only she wasn't such a procrastinator.

The first step in playing the game with Mavis is to understand why she is so indecisive. In her case, it seems, procrastination goes hand-in-hand with perfectionism. Mavis is literally handicapped by her need to be perfect in everything she does. She (and others similarly afflicted by chronic indecision) finds herself in a Catch-22 situation—compelled to accept any challenge (she would be less than perfect if she admitted there was some task beyond her competence) but unable to complete the job because of her need to make it perfect. Wafflers are competent and intelligent people. Their self-concept, however, is very much dependent on others seeing the perfect execution of everything they do.

This knowledge can help you deal with them. In most cases, you have to assist the Waffler in making the job appear perfect (or the decision easier). This means gathering the information necessary for the Waffler to make an informed (and thus "more perfect") decision or packaging the information in such a way that the Waffler will see it as perfect. For example, if a vacillating boss can't get around to doing your performance appraisal, it may be because an easily completed form does not exist and the thought of developing such a "perfect form" is too overwhelming.

A resourceful employee might choose to design the form himself and present it to the waffling boss as a way of moving the process forward. But things are not always as easy as they might seem. Perfectionists have a need to polish existing work. In this case, you might suggest that the boss use a form already in use elsewhere. Creativity and persistence lead ultimately to success.

REMORSEFUL WAFFLER

Audrey had always thought of her husband, Al, as quick and decisive. But she found the aftermath of his decision making to be frustrating. He would agonize over his decisions, sometimes for weeks. "Do you think I did the right thing?" he'd ask and then present a different scenario for her consideration: "What if I'd done it this way instead? Is it too late to change my mind?" And so on. Audrey listened patiently and tried to get him to see that he had indeed done the right thing. But it was starting to wear on her. She also knew there were times when Al's quick thinking did get him into trouble.

Al waffles after-the-fact. He seeks reassurance that he made the right decision. To play this game, Audrey needs to be less of a counsellor giving supportive feedback. Rather, she needs to firmly reassure him that he has made a good decision. That is, when he has. When she believes the decision is not sound, she should engage him in a practical, problem-solving discussion.

At no time should she attempt to commiserate on the situational factors, with his approach to the problem or his decision-making ability. "You're right, Al...that probably could have been done differently. But let's focus on what we've learned. Next time this situation occurs, how would you approach it?" She should add some positive reinforcement to counteract his insecurity, "I really admire you for your ability to use a mistake to improve the situation."

Don't wait for a Waffler to ask for your reassurance. Give it to him. Whenever he makes a decision, especially a major one, follow it up with a direct compliment: "I think that was a good decision," or (perhaps more indirectly) "Good thinking."

The objective in playing the game with Wafflers is to neither nurture nor reinforce this frustrating behaviour but rather, through patience and creativity, to initiate opportunities for making good decisions and then to validate those actions.

Recognize the contributing factors to the challenging behaviour. Counter them intelligently and with sensitivity. This is especially important if your boss happens to be the Waffler.

22 WHINERS

Be the solution, not the problem.

Whiners have an unrelenting need to tell us about all the things that have gone wrong in their lives as well as what we should be doing to correct them. Their constant carping is a problem for us simply because it never seems to be in their power to fix these concerns themselves. These players are big on problems but short on solutions.

Whiners see themselves as noble warriors for all that's right in the world, so they complain about all they see that's wrong. They are self-righteous folk who view themselves as perfect, but powerless. They typically have an answer or, better still, a prescription to virtually all of life's many problems but they assume they lack either the authority or the means to implement solutions. The act of whining keeps them blameless and innocent...in their own eyes at least.

Not surprisingly, Whiners crave attention. Depending on their sense of powerlessness, they can be overbearing. Indeed, once on a roll, they seem to find fault with everything. Sentences flow almost without pause, connected by a seemingly endless string of "ands" and "buts". Rarely is a single accusation the focus of their complaint. They seem to be saving up their complaints, waiting for an innocent victim to play their game. They are the "whine and jeez" people.

The first thing you have to do in playing the game with Whiners is to break their momentum. Interrupt them when they seem to be gaining momentum and ask for specifics. Although they prefer to generalize, when pressed, Whiners will often give you some details. Remember these; you will need to come back to specifics later. Beware that Whiners are adept at character assassination. Avoid entering into this kind of discussion at all costs, simply because you can't win and it's rarely germane to their complaints anyway.

Once you're able to get into the conversation, encourage them to outline the details of their complaints. Listen carefully as you will need this information to point a direction towards action, usually in the form of leading questions. *Your primary objective* in playing this game is to convince them that they are not powerless, that they are capable of dealing constructively with the problems they uncover. In dealing with Whiners, there is truth in the adage that you're either part of the problem or you're part of the solution.

Once you have a better understanding of the specifics of the problem or concern, ask the blamer for her constructive ideas and suggestions: "What solutions have *you* thought about?" Try to move the discussion toward problem solving. Ask questions about the details she provides. Ask for examples. Focus on alternatives and options before you start thinking about possible solutions. Should you receive an indication of a willingness to consider these possible approaches, assign limited tasks so that subsequent progress can be measured.

Anticipate the Whiner's favourite generalizations: *always* and *never.* Learn how to counter them with pointer questions. (A pointer question is one that points to or solicits specifics.) In this case, simply repeat his favourite response but in a questioning tone: "Always?" Use pointers as well when unfavourable comparisons are made: "Worse than what?"

Whiners need an audience. So listen to them, appear attentive and acknowledge their concerns. You can't play this game (or any game for that matter) if you alienate them at the outset by appearing to suggest that their concerns are not legitimate. Convey the impression that you are genuinely interested and that you do understand the seriousness of the problems they are bringing to your attention. Be patient but remain focused on your objective.

Do not agree with a Whiner, even if he happens to be right. The last thing you want to do is reinforce his perception of self-righteousness. Should you be the target of his complaining, never admit to wrongdoing—this will only serve to energize his self-concept of perfection. Rather, indicate that you will look into the matter or, if it happens to be an accurate observation about your behaviour, that you will think about it.

Whiners are fuelled by gossip and rumours. The problem is that second-hand information is rarely accurate; despite the best intention of the messenger, it invariably contains distortions. And, in the hands of a self-righteous blamer, rumours can sometimes take on sinister proportions. The best way to handle complaints born of gossip is to nip them in the bud: "I think you should know, Michelle, that I really don't put much stock in rumours." It may seem hard at times to resist a juicy piece of gossip but, unless you do, you're only reinforcing the Whiner's propensity to blame others for her problems.

TRIANGULAR COMPLAINING

Triangular complainers are people who complain to you about the behaviour of others. Despite the temptation, don't get sucked in to this game. Acknowledge his concern, but suggest that your experience with that person has been different: "Isn't it interesting that you would see her in that light; that's not been my experience." The point is a simple one: discussions about the behaviour of another person in her absence, when she can neither defend herself nor present the proper context for interpreting behaviour, are not productive. Nor are they fair.

Likewise, be careful when *you* use third-party sources to correct the Whiner's complaint or his perspective on the issue at hand. Whiners will typically, and perhaps correctly, insist that you identify your source of information, and compliance with that request will only jeopardize the willingness of colleagues to confide in you. Revealing your sources is surely not the point of the discussion anyway. So, when you are confronted with "Who told you that?", simply repeat the point you're trying to make, without attribution. Refocus the discussion on the issue, not on the source of your information: "John, the point is that your version may not be entirely accurate. What we are trying to discuss here is...."

If you happen to be the boss in this type of encounter, be wary of a trap Whiners will set. Upon entering into problem solving ("What do you think we can do about this problem?"), you may receive the artful retort: "Well, that's why I came to you. You're the boss, not me. You get paid to solve these problems; I don't."

Remember that this is a game. Stay focused on your primary objective. As with all the players, especially the really good ones, the Whiner's singular purpose, once cornered, is to put you on the defensive. Sure you're the boss. But does that mean you must have an answer for every problem? Even if that were the case, how would you encourage your subordinates to become independent problem solvers if they know you have all the answers? Don't be enticed by the trap, as tempting as it might appear. Use that same opportunity that has now been handed to you and stay on course: "That's right, I am the boss. That's why I want you to go back to your office, think about the situation, and then come back to me with some constructive ideas for resolving this problem. Better still, why don't you write me a memo with a list of possible solutions." The purpose, as always, is to get the problem finder involved in solution finding, not just in complaining.

While listening attentively to the complainant is generally a necessary and good first step in uncovering useful information and in getting the blamer to take some responsibility for finding possible solutions, you may not always have the time or the inclination to play out this part of the game. Mindful of tact, here's a short cut which you might use occasionally. Since you now know that the complainer's tirade invariably comes in an almost endless string of accusations, eventually (with your prompting) leading up to the *real* issue, you can easily short-circuit the conversation with the following question: "Where do you want to be at the end of this conversation, Ted?" It's an attention-grabber. And it will usually produce results. (It's also bullying behaviour and, used frequently, will give you a deserved reputation for abruptness.)

KEEPING COMPLAINERS AWAY

"Oh no, here she comes again," Jake said to himself as he caught sight of Elva heading towards his door. Elva was notorious for her boring tirades on the sad state of affairs of just about everything. She loved to complain and all she needed to get started was somebody's ear. It had reached the point where her colleagues were designing complex strategies to avoid her. But a new staff member, unaware of Elva's need for a good listener, had been trapped on several occasions, saving the rest of the staff from her tedious monologues about what was wrong with the world.

Unfortunately for the old-timers, the new fellow soon caught on and was now employing his own evasive tactics. Jake prepared himself as Elva made her rounds in search of another victim. It appeared to be his turn this morning. This time, he had a new strategy—one his teenage daughter told him had worked on a boyfriend who was "just like Elva." Before Elva could launch into her normal diatribe, Jake stood up and said, firmly and pleasantly, "Hello Elva. Before you tell me what's on your mind, I have to tell you I have 10 minutes before I have to leave for a meeting. Have a seat and tell me what's bothering you." For the next 10 minutes, Jake listened attentively, occasionally nodding to indicate his interest. He made a few notes when something sounded important. He stifled his normal impulse to interrupt and give her advice. (He had concluded long ago that Elva was not the least bit interested in his, or anybody's, advice. Whenever he had offered it in past, she either dismissed it or explained at length why his suggestions couldn't possibly work.)

After 10 minutes of listening and nodding, Jake looked at his watch, stood up, said "Excuse me. I have to leave for my meeting now." He then moved toward the door. When she looked surprised, he smiled and said pleasantly, "Thanks Elva for bringing these concerns to my attention. If you don't mind, we can carry on tomorrow. What time would be convenient for you?" Dumbfounded, Elva found her feet and, without another word, made her way out of his office. "That wasn't too bad," thought Jake. "It was painful inviting her back again tomorrow, but it could have been worse. I don't think I've ever got rid of her in under a half hour!"

Not surprisingly, Elva appeared at Jake's office again next morning. Jake followed the same routine as the day before, including an explicit reference to his time limitation. After their conversation, he again invited her back for a discussion the following day. After several days, Jake realized that these brief meetings weren't all that bad, especially as he no longer wasted his energy offering suggestions that Elva quickly rejected. In fact, he was beginning to enjoy this brief morning interlude. It had become an interesting and insightful game—an opportunity to examine his behaviour as much as hers. Not only was he in control of his time, he didn't have to subject himself to her complaining at other times in the day. If she did approach him in her whining mode, he would simply say, "Elva, this will have to wait until tomorrow morning. We can also discuss the Jackson project at that time." He noted as well that Elva was getting a little more focused on dealing with some of the issues she raised.

Jake's meetings with Elva continued for almost three weeks. Then, one Friday morning, she didn't appear at her scheduled time. As the morning passed, Jake ventured from his sanctuary and located her working at her typewriter. "Gee, Elva, I missed you this morning. What happened?" Looking sheepish, she explained, "Sorry, I just didn't have anything to tell you." Speechless, Jake retreated to his office to consider what he had just heard. He had won the game.

Had Elva run out of complaints? He needed to share this development with someone, so he paid a visit to the Office Manager, Natalie. She listened then added her observations. It seemed that she and other staff had noticed a difference in Elva as well. Most noteworthy was that her complaints about Jake had stopped. Her complaints in general had diminished and she was spending more time on her work and less time seeking out others to whom she could complain. Natalie assumed that since Elva now had Jake's ear every morning, she didn't need theirs anymore.

Six months later, Elva was still going into Jake's office to complain but now it was about one session a week. Jake concluded that his investment of time was a worthwhile tradeoff for increased staff morale, higher productivity and better work habits from Elva.

THE FACELESS COMPLAINER

As Grounds Supervisor at the university, Walter's job is to ensure the land-scaping and outside facilities are properly maintained and look presentable. His staff of 27 men and women are unionized. Walter has no problem doing his job; the big-gest challenge lies in handling complaints, particularly those received from the faculty. The more difficult ones come from those he calls "prima donnas." There are only a few of these grumblers but Walter knows their voices as soon as he picks up the phone.

Many of the complaints he receives are legitimate. Yesterday during the big snowstorm, for example, he had several complaints about the lack of parking spaces. This is normal when people get frustrated and it just wasn't possible for his crew to get all the snow removed before employees began arriving for work. But one of the calls had come from his least favourite blamer, Prof. Sims. He called to complain about the way the sidewalk in front of his office window had been shovelled.

Sims had one of those prestigious offices on the ground floor of the Economics building. When Walter asked about the nature of the problem, Sims explained that the cleared sidewalk was too narrow and, when students walked by two abreast, they would brush the snowbanks causing the snow to cascade down onto the freshly cleaned sidewalk. As more students walked by, these lumps of snow were trodden into a slick surface that made walking treacherous. Sims explained that the university would be liable should some poor soul fall down and injure herself. Nor did he want to have to trudge out into the weather to rescue anyone so unlucky. He had too much work to do anyway, what with all the cutbacks. He went on to describe several other unrelated concerns but ended by asking Walter to send someone over "right away" to deal with the problem.

It was at times like this when Walter wondered about a different career. If he could, he would just grab a shovel and hustle over and do the job himself. But he knew the union contract prohibited such initiative. He knew his workers took some short cuts on days such as this and that jobs weren't always performed to the standard he preferred.

Prof. Sims' sidewalk was added to the list of jobs for the snow crew. Unfortunately, the storm and the subsequent mess it had created around the university made this task such a low priority that it almost disappeared from the job list. Explaining to Sims that he would have someone attend to the problem "first thing in the morning" wasn't good enough for the professor. Sims then went into his whining lecture mode and complained at length about the loss of pride in one's job, the university being delinquent about safety matters, concern for the students, and so on.

Walter wished his own boss, Jack, would take an interest in dealing with the faculty. But that appeared to be a lost cause. Once Walter had approached Jack about Prof. Sims' complaining but he just laughed and said, "Walt, that's why I hired you. I've never been able to deal with those characters." So the task of reducing Sims' incessant whining to tolerable levels fell on Walter's shoulders. He had no choice but to play the game.

Sims is, by definition, a Whiner. Unfortunately for Walter, he is also in a position of power. So his complaining, more often than not, tends to take on an aggressive, bullying tone. Clearly, one of Walter's roles at the university is to provide support services to the faculty. So he needs to be tactful in how he approaches the impending game with Sims.

In dealing with complaints from people in authority, Walter could rely on the university's written policies and procedures for dealing with such special or unique situations. When Sims makes an unreasonable request, he could quote "Policy # 456, which refers to the prioritization of tasks in heavy snowfall conditions." Although a somewhat bureaucratic response, it might short-circuit Sims' constant complaints over minor concerns. It would certainly be in keeping with the culture of the organization—universities do have policies and procedures to cover just about every situation imaginable.

Walter might also consider whether or not his behaviour may have something to do with the complaining. In certain situations, he could be more assertive. He could learn to say "No" tactfully, without engaging in lengthy explanations (which Sims doesn't want to hear anyway). He could simply respond with a diplomatic refusal to put this job at the top of the priority list: "I'm sorry to hear about your problem. Unfortunately, we can't get there until tomorrow morning." The objective here is not to offend Sims; rather, it is to occasionally stand up to unrealistic expectations. Whiners like to complain to those who will do something about the complaints. They don't play the game with unresponsive people.

Walter may also want to consider the merits of occasionally putting a couple of "credits" in his personal account with Sims. Instead of dealing with the complaint over the phone, he might pay a personal visit to the professor and view the problem first-hand. In so doing, he would be giving Sims the recognition and acknowledgement he likely craves. The ensuing conversation would also give Walt a better opportunity to describe his point of view about such concerns. He could now focus on his objective and engage Sims in a problem-solving session.

"Gee, Prof. Sims, you know more about human behaviour than I do. How can I get my own staff motivated to do a better job? Because that's a big part of the problem here." With this more creative and collaborative approach, Sims may find it difficult to give Walter a hard time over the phone in future. It's difficult to be nasty or aggressive when you know the face that belongs to the voice. And Walter may just discover that, as a result of this personal encounter, some faculty aren't the prima donnas he suspects they are.

To play the game with a Whiner, you must first listen to their complaints. Don't agree with them, just acknowledge their concerns. Resist the temptation to either give advice or assume the responsibility for solving the problems they identify. Limit their complaints (either with time limits or by soliciting action on a particular concern). Encourage specifics. Find creative ways to induce them into problem solving. Empower them and teach them how to solve problems.

Before you engage a Whiner, keep in mind that some people do have legitimate complaints from time to time. They might raise serious concerns that warrant attention and collaborative resolution.

23 YES PEOPLE

Confirm the commitment.

Yes People are those wonderfully compliant and sweet folks who never seem to want to displease us but who typically do just that, by failing our every request. They are the "superagreeables," the ones who lead us to believe they are in total agreement with our ideas and requests only to let us down when we need them.

These friendly and willing types rarely follow through on their promises, largely because they make unrealistic commitments. The reason for this failure to deliver is that their compliant nature stems from a basic desire to be accepted and liked or loved by everyone, all of the time. This, of course, is an impossibility. Nonetheless, it is the goal they strive to achieve in their relationships.

To compound the difficulty, Yes People are usually terrified by the open confrontation that ensues from our annoyance with their inability to deliver on commitments. As a consequence, we don't quite know how to convey our frustration without upsetting them even more. And who among us would want to deliberately upset such nice people? Once again, the dilemma about how to deal with challenging behaviour is ours, not theirs.

Some use the pejorative label "Wimp" to typecast Yes people. Others, more kindly, describe them as passive (and, in some cases, passive-aggressive). Normally found in subordinate positions, they can be manipulative. Call it manipulation by the weak, if you wish. They do this by seeking our compassion for those who seem incapable of standing up for themselves. It is perhaps a function of a society founded largely on Christian values and the human tendency to help the underdog. Whatever the reason for our emotional response, their unproductive actions serve only to frustrate our best efforts to get the job done. We obviously can't fight with them, so instead we capitulate. In doing so, we reinforce their wimpish, overly-compliant behaviours.

MAKE IT EASY TO SAY NO

To play the game with Yes People, you start by reassuring them that your friendship or approval is not at stake. You must remind yourself that, in their eyes, compliant and agreeable behaviour is a fail-safe approach to gaining your approval and, in some cases, your affection. After all, through the years they learned this lesson well in their dealings with parents and other authority figures. So you must tell them

156

the obvious: "Good friends don't always see eye-to-eye *on everything*, John." While none would deny its validity, superagreeables must hear that message often.

In playing this game, don't be sidetracked from your primary objective by their frequent use of self-deprecating humour and personal put-downs. The purpose of such tactics is to make you more accepting of them. That's precisely the point: it is done with a purpose, whether consciously or not. It's a favourite response because it has worked so effectively in the past. Belittling themselves is by now an *unthinking reaction* to those whom they seek to please. Expect the put-down but counter it appropriately: "That's just not true, John, and I think you know that." If Yes People are incapable of attending to their own self-esteem, you must provide the structure for them to do so.

Here is where the struggle begins. The harder you try to reassure them that their self-criticism is either wrong or misplaced, the more likely it is they will disagree with your viewpoint. But you are making progress. Stop the conversation at this point and interject: "John, you're disagreeing with me. And there's nothing wrong with that. Now let's get back to the matter at hand."

This is your principle objective to get them to disagree with you without eliciting your retaliation or disapproval. Your purpose is to make it easy for them to say "no." You can do this in different ways. Give them the benefit of an excuse: "Might there be any problem in getting that job done by Friday, John? I know that you're awfully busy these days." Now wait and listen attentively. Show him you're interested, not disappointed, in what he has to say now that you've provided him the opportunity to disagree.

Once you know what you need to do, choose appropriate language. You want to induce the desired perception and, eventually, modify this behaviour. This is the essence of the game. You must not only know your objective, you must know how to get started and what to say in response to their ingrained defensive responses. Here are a few more tactful methods for dealing with Yes People.

Anticipate and learn how to counter their favourite expressions—sayings like "*No problem*" or "*I'll try my best*." Experience has told you that these responses are early warning signals. You want a commitment, something concrete on which you can follow up should there subsequently be a problem. Tell the superagreeable in an honest and sincere fashion: "Sorry, John, but that's just not good enough. I need a commitment."

Never accept vague or general promises from Yes People, as in their usual "okay" response. *The more abstract their promise, the easier is their escape* from the responsibility of following through. Always get the details (and the more specific, the better). Here is an example: "So I can expect it on my desk later this week?"

"Sure, no problem."

"On Thursday or Friday?"

"I don't know...Friday probably."

"Morning or afternoon, John?"

This may appear to be stretching the point. But remind yourself who you're dealing with. You've experienced this evasive promise before. His "commitments" in the past have not led to action. If he protests your concern for minutiae, tell him it's important to you or the organization and *that's* why you need the details. Give him your sense of urgency or priority.

When you finally do get a specific commitment ("Okay, I'll have it on your desk by 11 o'clock, Friday morning."), it's not a bad idea to confirm it even further: *Then I have your word on that?* Overkill? Maybe. But your objective, as always, is to change habitual behaviour. In so doing, you'll need an arsenal of proven tactics and remarkable patience.

Don't let Yes People make promises you know they cannot possibly keep. You're only asking for trouble if you do. Be prepared to compromise on your demands in order to ensure follow-through on the task at hand. A word of caution: if the task really is important to you or the organization, it may be wise to get someone else to do it. In some situations, prudence and experience pays.

MANAGING COMPLIANT BOSSES

What if your boss is one of the Yes People? While it's somewhat unusual for superagreeables to rise to positions of power and authority, there are exceptions to every rule. If it does happen, your best approach is to stress the consequences of his lack of follow-through, either for you or for the organization. "I want to do a good job for you, Bob, but when these things happen I really can't do my best work." This is a consequence that every boss should be able to appreciate.

By focusing on corporate responsibilities, he may soon discover that the relationship is not in jeopardy but your performance and productivity surely are. Although subordinates rarely do so, inviting constructive criticism from an overly agreeable superior is really an effective way of managing the boss. "I know my report's not perfect, Bob. And it would really help us get new business if I could improve on my presentation format. Can you give me some pointers?"

If you lack the inclination or if the circumstances seem inappropriate, there is an alternative to an open confrontation with Yes People. You can leave a note clearly expressing your expectations: "I want this done by noon on Friday. If there's any reason why it can't be done, please let me know by Thursday afternoon at the latest.

Thanks." What this approach lacks in courage it may accomplish in effectiveness.

Of course, it's hard to imagine that such warm, friendly and nice people could be labelled as challenging players. But, as with all these frustrating types, their behaviour lacks balance. The problem is that they are *always* friendly and nice. They are unwilling either to say "no" or to compromise even when the situation warrants their disagreement or when their ability to comply with our requests is virtually non-existent.

The best therapy you can offer Yes People is to create a non-threatening presence, become an empathic listener and reassure them that "no" is not a dirty word.

24 THE ESSENCE

Rapport makes all things possible.

It is said that first impressions are lasting impressions. Common sense aside, a considerable body of research verifies this timeless conclusion. In 1979, American psychiatrist Leonard Zunin noted that the first four minutes of any encounter are critical to "making or breaking" a lasting impression. Others claim this crucially important first impression is formed much earlier, within seconds in some cases. Another study suggests that 90% of your lasting impression is formed in the first 90 seconds of the encounter.

Whatever the research suggests, it doesn't take long to make an almost indelible impression. During those dynamic initial seconds and minutes that can be crucial to the future of a relationship, we simultaneously project and receive these impressions. Yet rarely are we aware of the significance of our words or body language in establishing that vital first assessment.

It must be evident by now that your success in the game of life is largely dependent on how others perceive you. So why leave it to chance? Take the view that creating a positive first impression is a critical skill you must develop if you are to have a tactical advantage in whatever game you play. The ability to "bond" with others requires an understanding of alignment and translation.

We align with those who appear to understand our needs. Indeed, as demonstrated, acknowledging one's needs is critical to winning the game. Needs not only motivate us to take action, they represent our vulnerabilities or "soft spots." We are more likely to convince others when we deliver our message in a way that appeals to their needs, not ours.

Translation acknowledges that no two people speak the same "language." Even though it might appear that we are speaking the same language, we do so with unique personal variations. We use pet phrases, we use words imprecisely and we use jargon and acronyms. Our language is a reflection of our individual "cultures".

Translation is listening to the other person's language in order to communicate our thoughts and ideas in words they can understand. When we translate effectively, people understand what we're trying to tell them, they assimilate it more readily and, in some cases, they are genuinely motivated by our message. All because we take the time necessary to understand and translate it back into their language. The result, especially in a conflict situation, can be almost magical.

Alignment and translation require both non-verbal and verbal communications skills. How we dress and behave, our mannerisms and gestures, all convey meaning. And we are more likely to accept the meaning from someone who is similar to ourselves. Who do you consider to be the most well-informed people in the world today? The answer is probably those who think and act as you do. This illustrates the power of translation and alignment.

Your effectiveness in aligning and translating yourself speaks to your ability to create trust, which is critical to your success. When people trust you, they tell you what you need to know. They give you quality information. When there is distrust, the information you need to play effectively is insufficient, inaccurate or, in some cases, fraudulent.

A positive and lasting impression can be created by consciously exhibiting the following behaviours in your initial encounters with people. Together, they add up to a winning combination. They help people to *like* you. They make them want to align with your needs or, at least, not immediately resist them.

Perhaps the most important gesture in encouraging bonding behaviour is the ability to smile. Not a false "put-on" smile, but one that's genuine. Equally important is the ability to make eye contact. Like smiling, eye contact creates an instant impression of liking and interest. Those who avert their gaze are perceived as lacking credibility. Worse, this can convey an impression of submissiveness or guilt. Some people have difficulty making eye contact. By gazing directly into another's eyes, they feel they're staring. The skill, instinctive for some, is to focus on an area near the eyes. What's important is not where you look but that the other person perceives you to be making eye contact.

The use of open-ended questions is another social bonding technique. Asking questions encourages the other person to talk and permits them the space to elaborate. Most people like to talk about themselves. So encourage them to do so, especially in that critical first meeting. As curious as it may seem, the more you allow people to talk about themselves, the more they will like you.

In a casual and subtle way, lean towards the other person. This supportive non-verbal body posture gives the impression you are sincerely interested (in what they have to say and therefore in who they are). It indicates to them that you are indeed listening to what they have to tell you. A knowledge of the importance of interpersonal distances is also important. Each of us has a sense of our preferred spaces of intimacy, respect and deference. Knowing the difference between proper social distance and the intimate zone can help you create the right initial impression, especially when dealing with people of other cultures.

Dress is also an important consideration, especially in business situations. I am not proposing "power dressing"; rather, I advocate common-sense apparel—clothing that is appropriate for the occasion. This too is a form of alignment. The object is to use your dress to competitive advantage, not to make a declaration of independence. Don't let your ego get in the way of your objectives.

Lastly, names and titles are important to people. Get them on first meeting people, get them right and use them often. It is advisable to use a formal title (Mr. or Mrs. Jones) unless or until you're advised not to do so. This is especially important with your seniors. If remembering names is not one of your better skills, simply ask the other person to repeat his name, then repeat it one more time to yourself.

Incorporating these skills into your game repertoire will ensure your first impression is a lasting one.

INTERACTION CYCLES

Generally speaking, there are only two ways to deal with others. We can act rationally or we can react emotionally. It is a choice we must make if we are to play the game well. When we react without thinking, we go on the offensive and attack, criticize or reaccuse. Or we become defensive. As we defend our position (or our identity), our behaviour and words become exaggerated and intense. This defensive behaviour is counterproductive and self-defeating.

If we decide to act in a rational manner, to think before doing, a wide variety of strategic options are available. And our subsequent actions will more likely be in keeping with our objectives. This is what winning is all about.

Whenever we encounter others, we engage in a perception-reaction dynamic. How I perceive and react to you is a consequence of how you perceive and react to me. We rarely "think" about this interaction. We quickly take in information and react as we have done in similar situations with other similar people.

For example, if someone called you a jerk, how would you likely react? What would you say? Would you retaliate by calling her a similar name? Then, no doubt, upon hearing your verbal assault, she would escalate the conflict by slinging a further insult at you.

Why would you have reacted in this manner? Because it's human nature to defend oneself in the face of a perceived attack on one's self-image. It's instinctive to counterattack. Almost subconsciously, we are seeking to "even up the score." In doing so, we tend to hit back a little harder, usually by adding a further insult to our response. Our message in this case is "Don't try that again." Defending oneself from this perceived threat and counterattacking is an emotional response. It's also the reason why most minor conflicts escalate in an unthinking, uncontrolled way.

If, during such an encounter, you had the presence of mind to *stop and think* of a more appropriate response, the potential for conflict would be held in check. Consider a more rational response to the "I think you're a jerk!" remark. Following a momentary pause to control your instinctive urge to counterattack, a better tactical response would be something like this: "You may be right about that, Charlie. Now getting back to our problem...." At this point in the confrontation, your attacker's options have been limited. He could persist but, since he's not receiving a response in kind, he will soon look (and feel) rather silly. Furthermore, his attack will subside as he vents whatever emotion may have caused it in the first place.

CONFLICT REQUIRES COOPERATION

Conflict is fundamentally an act of cooperation. It is sustained when each antagonist supports and energizes the other by counterassaults. Conversely, a thinking response, admittedly more difficult to achieve than shooting back from the lip, will de-escalate conflict and enable you to take control of the confrontation.

Understanding the perception-reaction dynamic is fundamental to playing the game successfully. This is so because we have a natural predisposition to filter our encounters with people through our past experiences. We perceive and react to stereotypical behaviours rather than seeing the other person with fresh eyes and a thinking mind every time we meet. We do not look for insights that highlight the individualism of the people with whom we play the game. We do not benefit from our awareness of player prototypes. Rather, we allow ourselves to be creatures of habit and we react accordingly.

When we encounter challenging players, we react to their tactics largely in accordance with how we feel at the moment. We react emotionally. We do what we feel we are "supposed to do" under the circumstances. Therein lies their success. When we deal with the silent, unresponsive type, for example, we become impatient and frustrated. Then we walk out, wondering why we even bothered trying to communicate with them. In so doing, we only succeed in reinforcing their strategy. The Oyster discovers once again that, if he waits us out, we'll quit the game. And we rarely disappoint his expectation.

We all learned how to play our games as coping strategies for dealing with difficult situations and difficult people. Our tactics were devised, honed and reinforced through successive encounters with the other players in our games. Think about it. Don't we all play our own games whenever we need to avoid stressful situations, disarm, outmanoeuvre or, in some cases, punish others? Don't we occasionally play games to satisfy our needs and achieve our objectives? Invariably, we are successful, especially when we encounter an unthinking opponent—someone who can't figure out the game.

Tactics that work in the game of life rely on unthinking responses. These tactics include the litany of confusing and offensive behaviours already described. They are, however, unsuccessful in the presence of thinking players. Because their responses effectively counter, constructively influence and ultimately modify the challenging behaviour. Thinking responses enable us to use the perception-reaction dynamic to our advantage.

NEGATIVE INTERACTION CYCLES

A failure to recognize the perception-reaction dynamic inevitably leads relationships toward a negative interaction cycle. This is a mutually reinforcing cycle of negative perception (or anticipation) followed by negative reaction followed by increasingly negative perceptions. And so it goes—down into the depths of frustration, anger and despair.

Tom Dryden listens nervously as he is introduced to an audience of his peers at the annual sales conference. He has never given this presentation before and, given the importance of this audience to his career, he nervously shuffles his notes. The knowledge that his boss' superiors are also sitting in the audience doesn't help. Finally, the introduction is over and he approaches the podium to polite but reserved applause. He adjusts the microphone and it screeches back. He clears his throat.

In the middle of his opening ice-breaker, Tom notices two people in the third row whispering to each other. He looks away, concentrating on the story that flowed so smoothly after his many rehearsals. He glances back to the twosome in row three. Now they're covering their mouths in an effort to stifle laughter. And Tom hasn't reached the punch line. He feels flushed and, aware of the beads of sweat on his forehead, he "flubs" the story. When he finally reaches the punch line, there are a few polite chuckles but mostly Tom looks out at friendly stares. He clears his throat again, searching to find his place. A page is not where it should be. The audience starts to fidget; a few conversations begin here and there. Tom no longer has their attention and he knows it. From this point forward, things go from bad to worse.

When Tom perceived (or, more likely, anticipated) a negative response from his audience, he reacted in a self-defeating mode. This reaction was reciprocated by his audience, thus confirming his initial perception. As he lost control over his well-rehearsed presentation, he lost control of his audience. His perceptions were self-fulfilling and thus virtually impossible to reverse.

The longer a conflict ensues between any two antagonists, the more they will come to resemble one another in their behaviours and their tactics. Once a negative interaction cycle is established, it can be almost impossible to break. With the passage of time, the solution is often bitter separation, followed by remorse or revenge.

Tom's encounter with his audience illustrates this classic interaction cycle. Tom incorrectly perceived that the audience was aware of his nervousness. As a result, he began to project his nervousness. The conversation in the third row was an unrelated event, and certainly not about Tom. But he chose to see it as confirmation that they knew of his problem. And it negatively affected his subsequent performance to the degree that his nervousness increased and eventually became obvious to everyone. When this happened, so too did the inevitable: he bombed.

More constructively, a positive interaction cycle could have been created. Let's examine a different scenario for Tom's presentation: he listens carefully to his intro-duction in anticipation of getting to the podium. He has spent long hours creating this presentation and he knows it will be on the mark for this audience. It's also a wonderful opportunity to impress his boss' superiors whom he understands are in the audience. He's been waiting for just such an opportunity for quite some time.

Tom gets to the podium and immediately thanks his introducer for her flat-tering remarks. He smiles at the audience and begins with his favourite lead-in story, one he's used before many times. He knows it will deliver the same results: gales of laughter. He isn't disappointed. The audience is now his. He checks his notes and pushes them aside. Tom feels comfortable and energetic. He knows his stuff. And the audience responds, attentively, with positive non-verbal feedback. At the end of his remarks, he confidently asks for questions and at least a dozen hands shoot up. A successful presentation. Tom revels in the good feeling.

In playing the game, you must address and arrest any negative thoughts you might have about the encounter. Both before and during the game, you must *stop and think*. By acknowledging and taking control of your normal emotional tendencies and by reacting in a different, more positive way, you can exert the influence necessary to get others to modify and, ultimately, change their tactics.

Perhaps you're wondering how you can translate this great theory into useful practice. Here is a practical tool for regaining your composure when the game becomes intense. Like all tools, this one requires practice before it can be mastered. It takes practice to change old habits. Which is precisely what your normal, un-thinking response patterns happen to be. (Acknowledging that these responses aren't working to your advantage is an important first step.)

THE PCV VALVE

A valve is a mechanism of control, one that can be used to dissipate built-up pressure. What if you could activate such a valve in the presence of a challenging player, especially one who is adept at pushing your hot buttons? Its purpose would be to make you a thinking player. PCV is an acronym for Pause, Control and Value.

Suppose you are confronted with the following: "Kristen, don't you ever think? Look what you've done. You've ruined this project." Your instinctive reaction might be an emotion-laden defence. Instead, do nothing. Pause for a moment. This is the momentary but necessary break in what would otherwise be an unthinking response. Indeed, perhaps an outburst. Three seconds is sufficient; five seconds would be better. The hardest thing to do in a confrontation such as this is to do nothing. But you're not doing nothing. You're taking control of yourself. You are also beginning to take control of the encounter.

If you think this is tough to do, then practice is the only way to increase your comfort. Remind yourself in different ways, perhaps before an anticipated confrontation, that you will take this momentary pause when things get heated. The more you do it, and the more you feel the power of self-control, the more comfortable and competent you will be with this tool.

During this initial pause, you've also begun a necessary thought process. In a microsecond, you should be asking yourself a few simple questions, like: *Why am I feeling this way?* And *Why is she saying that to me?* These are two essential questions we rarely contemplate when we're under attack. But, if you give yourself the time to think about them, the answers will enable you to take control of the perception-reaction dynamic.

Exactly what is it that you are controlling? Your words, tone of voice and body language. Don't raise your voice. Keep it at the same level of intonation as before the accusation. When you shout back, your accuser feels legitimized. He can now shout again. There may be occasions when you might want to lower your voice slightly, thus inducing a perception of the seriousness of your concern. But never raise your voice; doing so will only sustain and energize the anger of the other person.

You must also control your non-verbal responses. *All of you is communicating.* Look at the other person with an open expression, using your eyes, face and body. Holding your palms open and upward expresses your sincerity and begs the question: "What's happening here?" Be wary of conveying a mixed message; you want your non-verbal message to be consistent with your verbal message. You want him to see that you are sincerely concerned.

Now it's time for you to value the other person. A good response would be to say: "I can understand why you would say that." (because no two people would say the same thing about that in any case). Or you might say: "I can appreciate why you would feel that way." What counts is how your comment is received, not what you may be thinking.

Understanding is not agreeing. Seeking to understand the legitimacy of another's values and perceptions does not compromise your views or your integrity. A valuing statement is essential in any confrontation with a challenging player. It serves to stop the unthinking perception-reaction dynamic. It allows you the necessary time to take control of yourself and your emotions (and hence your reactions). When you can do this, you begin to take control of the game.

Your ability to do these things—make a positive and lasting first impression, utilize the perception-reaction dynamic to advantage, control yourself in pressure situations and be a thinking player—will enable you to establish rapport with any player. Therein lies the essence of the game.

25 WINNING

Choose the right tools.

Like it or not, *whatever you do in life*, you require the cooperation of others. Whenever you seek to achieve personal or professional goals, exchange ideas, change attitudes, influence decisions, reach an agreement or seek to enhance the quality of your relationships, you invariably must turn conflict into cooperation. Knowing *"how to"* do that, how to find creative solutions when others oppose your views, makes life a lot simpler, less stressful, and more rewarding.

The game of life has been going on for countless centuries. It will continue to be played out by humankind whenever we desire to satisfy our needs and resolve our differences. The game consists of finite principles and infinite variables. It is a game of power, creativity and communication. It demands a delicate mixture of psychology and philosophy, of art and science, of style and substance. It prizes intuition as highly as intellect, common sense as much as inviolate norms. Some learn to play the game masterfully. Others only dimly understand it.

It should come as no surprise that an understanding of human behaviour is essential if you are to effectively play the game to the best of your ability. Although each of us is a unique human being, much of our behaviour is predictable. Capturing that predictability and codifying it into a set of explicit principles and useful insights has been the purpose of my book. This knowledge will be to your distinct advantage in the game of life, whatever your profession, your calling or your personal goals.

Although life may not be a game, the concept serves as a useful metaphor for understanding some of the complexities of human interaction. And it makes them slightly less intimidating. If you don't understand the basic principles of the game, you can't solve your problems, get your work done or advance your interests. If you don't accept the premise that life can be a game, you may not discover happiness in your relationships.

CREATURES OF HABIT

It is critical to your mental health, your growth and your vitality as a human being to acknowledge the power of habits. Over time, these unthinking responses become "boxes"—safe places in which to hide. Worse, when we lock ourselves inside these boxes, we become captive to our unique cultures. And, when that happens, we do not see what is occurring in our relationships.

Every player in the game of life is a unique human being, a product of his or her individual culture. She is not a product of your culture. His box is not yours. If you are to play the game well, you must appreciate that frame of reference. Without it, you cannot use conflict to foster cooperation.

Think back to your primary school years. Do you remember what mattered most? What were your hopes? What were your fears? What were your teachers' (or your parents') expectations of you? *Things are different now.* The culture of the school system—a powerful influence on human behaviour to be sure—has changed radically.

According to a CBS news report, the top seven elementary school problems in the 1960's were as follows:

1.   Talking out of turn.
2.   Chewing gum.
3.   Making noise in class.
4.   Running in the halls.
5.   Cutting into line.
6.   Dress code infractions.
7.   Littering.

Those who were part of that culture might have been guilty on all counts. Such infractions were easily survived. Now, guess what the top seven elementary school problems are in the 1990's?

1.   Drug abuse.
2.   Alcoholism.
3.   Pregnancy.
4.   Depression and suicide.
5.   Rape.
6.   Robbery.
7.   Assault.

If anything, this should give you a perspective on a culture that influences the behaviours of younger players with whom you have or will soon play the game. Different cultures produce different behaviours. Being sensitive to these differences will help unshackle your habitual creature and encourage you to think of more appropriate, artful and intelligent tactics. Utilize this knowledge to your advantage rather than continuing to fight their unique personal styles. Get out the box of unthinking responses before it seals you in.

Whenever you are confronted with challenging or puzzling behaviour in the game of life, pause for a moment and reflect on the notion that the other player is responding from a cultural bias or habit, rather than in a deliberate and premeditated fashion. This awareness alone will make you a better, and certainly more intelligent, player.

In the game of life, opposites do not attract. Each of us has a unique personality structure. The reason why you find some people to be challenging is because of *your* personality structure, not theirs. The players you are most likely to dislike are those who are the least like you. Moreover, the people to whom you react emotionally are those you like the least. Thus, to be successful, you must learn how to translate yourself and your needs to others. When you discover that the other player is "an opposite", and their dislike button is aroused by your very presence, it's time to start translating. If you don't (or if you can't), you've become a captive in your box of habitual responses. And you're going to lose the game once more.

PROCESS

When we play the game, our natural predisposition is to focus on isolated events rather than on the process of relationship building and enhancement. Those who understand the importance of process realize that win-win is a long-term investment; they focus on mutual profit improvement. Win-lose, conversely, is a short-term consideration. The objective is winning at the expense of the other person and, typically, at the expense of the relationship. Win-lose is a short-term gain in exchange for long-term pain.

While we may all intellectually appreciate these differences, win-lose too frequently is the instinctive response. We get into this mode when we don't stop and think. Any fool can be a win-lose player. And be aware that your motives are easily misinterpreted. Sometimes people perceive a win-lose outcome even though your intentions are win-win. Playing the game with those who have less power, like your children or subordinates, is a case in point.

A process orientation will help you become a better player. Conflict is a cooperative process. Influence is a trial and error process, with methods as varied as the people involved. Negotiating is an artful process wherein slow and dumb is often better than quick and smart. Communication is a process that requires you first to understand before you can be understood. The essence of these critical skills lies largely in your ability to understand the concept of process.

What counts in life are not the quantum leaps—which are soon found to be counterproductive and frustrating—but the small, incremental steps each of us can take in our daily lives toward constructive change and personal growth. (This is why I often refer to my workshops as "shoe stores." I invite the participants to shop , for those things that comfortably "fit" their personal needs, styles and situations.) Those who want to understand everything very quickly forget most of it. They frustrate themselves striving for perfection.

TOOLS

To succeed in the game of life, we need a few basic tools. And, since life is a matter of strategic choices, the choice of tools is up to you. These tools are like maps, compasses and flashlights. Maps give us a better sense of "the big picture"—where we are relative to where we want to be. Like aerial photography, they provide a clear view of alternative routes for reaching our chosen destination. The compass provides us with a sense of direction and tells us where to begin the journey. Flashlights help illuminate the darkness and complexity we will encounter along the way.

"The game" is also a basic tool. Its purpose is to help us see more clearly the context of our relationships and our objectives in important personal encounters. Knowing the motivations and tactics of the more challenging players ensures that our needs will not be easily subjugated to theirs. Understanding the rules brings predictability, comfort and confidence to our daily encounters.

The real challenge in getting better in the game of life lies not in acquiring new tools, but in letting go of unproductive ones. Too often we look for ways to make this learning easy, rather than searching for useful concepts that make us stop and think. We fail to acknowledge that we do not grow by knowing all the answers; we do so by living with the tough questions.

Maybe the secret to understanding the game of life lies in learning the value of the pregnant pause. Benjamin Hoff once wrote (in an obscure little book called "The Tao of Pooh"): "The masters of life know the way. They listen to the voice within them, the voice of wisdom and simplicity, the voice that reasons beyond cleverness and knows beyond knowledge. That voice is not just the power or property of a few, but has been given to everyone."

When you master the tool that enables you to stop and think, you will hear that voice. When you take that vital moment in the game of life to listen to yourself, you will think of more intelligent and appropriate tactical responses. You will become a better player.

In observing people attempt to learn how to use these basic tools, I am reminded of a story that belongs, I believe, to Stephen Covey. It's about a walker in the woods who came across a farmer seeking to cut down a large tree. After watching the farmer struggle for more than an hour at the same task, he made the following suggestion: "I am sure the job would go much faster were you to take a break and sharpen the saw."

"I can't," said the farmer. "I don't have time. I'm just too busy sawing." To become more skilled in the game of life, we must occasionally take a break and sharpen our saws.

WINNING

Those who succeed in the game of life are those who have discovered how to benefit from human nature, not those who continue to fight it. Sun Tzu, the military genius, has said: "The best general is the one who never fights." Edmund Burke, the philosopher, offered this sage wisdom: "He that wrestles with us strengthens our nerves and sharpens our skills. Our antagonist is our helper." It's an interesting point of view. It is the view of winners.

Putting the principles and ideas in this book to work for you on a daily basis will go a long way toward helping you win your game. They will help you eliminate the resistance, resentment and wasted effort you've experienced whenever you've had to confront one of the more challenging players. The objective of the game is to create productive, harmonious and mutually-rewarding relationships, without the counter-productive conflict and unnecessary stress that too often drain our energy, patience and talent.

Becoming a better player is more than an intellectual exercise. If you want to win more consistently, you have to change your approach to the game. We cannot achieve different results by continuing to do the same things. We cannot become what we want to be by remaining what we are. Les Brown, the black activist and entrepreneur, puts it this way: "If you want to do something you've never done before, you've got to be willing to become someone you've never been before." In short, you have to make some choices. And your success as a player will be entirely dependent on the quality of those choices.

For well over two decades, I have been teaching people from all walks of life how to improve their personal and professional lives through better negotiating skills. Those who subsequently improved their winning percentage, I'm convinced, fundamentally changed the way they negotiated. They changed their point of view about the process. They no longer saw negotiating as problem solving but rather as opportunity finding. They made a conscious choice to negotiate differently. Hence, the objective for them is no longer getting less by cutting their losses, but getting more by optimizing their gains.

You too will become a better player in the game when you make a personal commitment to change your habitual way of trying to resolve differences with others, when you adjust your attitude about how to get people to see it your way. Dennis Kimbro recently wrote the following about attitude:

The longer I live, the more I realize the impact of attitude on life. Attitude, to me, is more important than facts. It is more important than the past, than education, than money, than circumstances, than failures, than successes, than what other people think or say or do. It is more important than appearance, giftedness or skill. It will make or break a company, a church, a home. The remarkable thing is we have a choice every day regarding the attitude we will embrace for that day. We cannot change our past. We cannot change the fact that people will act in a certain way. We cannot change the inevitable. The only thing we can do is play on the one string we have and that is our attitude. I am convinced that life is 10% what happens to me and 90% how I react to it. And so it is with you...we are in charge of our ATTITUDE.

The key to *your* future lies entirely in your intentions. If you truly *intend* to do something, the likelihood of following through is great. Make a commitment, right now. Promise yourself that this will not be yet another one of those interesting self-help books. Having invested your precious time, tell yourself this: *the idea* of The Game of Life *can make a real difference in the quality of my well being.* That choice is yours to make.

You will not remember all of the principles, tactics and rules espoused in these pages. But you can change your point of view about how you will subsequently play the game. You can start seeing your encounters with these challenging people as opportunities and adventures, not as problems and frustrations. That choice is yours also.

Mark Twain once told of a young man who had a singular quest. He wanted to find the greatest general who ever lived. He wanted to sit down and talk with him. At first, he found time on weekends to pursue his goal. When it became an obsession, he journeyed further afield to fulfil his dream. Eventually, he left his vocation, his family and his town and dedicated himself solely to the pursuit of this great general.

Wherever he went, he met disappointment. He was occasionally encouraged, as when he was told that he had just missed this seemingly elusive traveller. One day, he came close and his pain was great. Upon asking, he was told that the general had been located a fortnight ago but that he had died in his sleep.

A life's quest is precisely that. The searcher waited out his time. When he died, he went to Heaven and was greeted at the pearly gates by St. Peter. He once again posed his question: "Do you know I have spent my entire life in search of but one thing?" St. Peter, being omniscient, answered, "Yes, I know. And your search is over. He's been waiting for you these many years. He's standing just over there. Go and have your talk with him, my son."

At first, the young man stared in excitement and anticipation. Then, upon recognizing the distant figure, he was crestfallen. He looked at St. Peter and, in a voice of desperation, said "There must be some mistake. I know that man. But he was a cobbler, not a general. He made shoes for a living."

St. Peter responded. "That is true. But if he had chosen to be a general, he would have been the greatest general who ever lived."

The story helps to remind us of the importance of making the right choices in the game of life. Generals are those who genuinely seek to master the game and play it artfully. Cobblers, on the other hand, spend their lives in sheer frustration, doing the same thing day in and day out—just pounding on a lot of shoe leather.

Which do you want to be? A general or a cobbler? The choice is entirely yours.

When you know how to play the game, you will experience life with greater intensity than ever before. Knowing the important principles and the unwritten rules will enable you to play masterfully, with grace and style. In time, through practice and commitment, we can all win and prosper in the game of life.

About the Author

Jim Murray is CEO of **optimal solutions** *international,* a virtual company that specializes in helping organizations and people reach their full potential. He is a rare breed. He holds four degrees, teaches at several Canadian and American universities, is a much sought-after advisor on corporate renewal, has over 25 years experience as a strategic planner, is an author, business columnist, professor of international law, labour relations mediator, and the list goes on.

During his eclectic career, Jim built four disparate organizations into success stories before purposefully moving on to new challenges. At every plateau, he redefined how business was done by focusing his intellect and energy squarely on his five principles for success: people, perspective, philosophy, paradox and persuasion.

As educator and transformational thinker, Jim has conveyed his views to hundreds of thousands of people from all walks of life through his seminars, books and business columns. Whether in Fortune 500 boardrooms or in the classroom, he has demonstrated his capacity to motivate people to change.

It is this same commitment and vision that led him to write *The Game of Life,* a "labour of love" that took over 10 years to complete. A father of four, Jim lives in Guelph, Ontario, and uses his thinking time to till the soil at his northern farm retreat.

ORDER DIRECT
by mail, fax or e-mail

The first edition of *The Game of Life* is available by direct order only. All orders must be prepaid. Enquire about discounts on bulk orders.

Ship to (please print name): _____

Complete Address: _____

_____
        (City)   (Prov./State)   (Zip/Postal Code)

Payment: By cheque/money order ☐   or   VISA ☐

                  Card number _____

                  Expiry_____Day telephone_____

                  Signature _____

To order via e-mail, visit our Web site at *http://www.the-game-of-life*.

Cost per book:

In Canada: $24.95
(with shipping and GST included, enclose $29.95 CDN)

In the U.S.: $17.95
(with shipping included, enclose $21.95 US)

Signed *First Edition* hardcover copy (limited quantity available):
$32.95 CDN + GST (shipped: $39.95)
$22.95 US (shipped $27.50)

For further information or bulk orders, contact the publisher:
optimal solutions *international*
28 Oxford St., Guelph Ont., N1H 2M3   Fax: 519-837-3446
Telephone: 519-837-0737   E-mail: optimal@sentex.net

THE GAME OF LIFE

Turning Conflict into Cooperation

Dr. James G. Murray

optimal solutions international
Guelph, Canada

Cover design by Global Marketing Services.
Page layout and assembly by Ampersand Printing.
Printed in Canada by Allprint Ainsworth Associates Inc.

First printing: February, 1998.

Canadian Cataloguing in Publication Data

Murray, James G. (James Gibson)
   The game of life: turning conflict into cooperation

ISBN 0-9680627-0-9

1. Interpersonal conflict. 2. Conflict management.
   I. Title.

BF637.S8M87 1997   158.2   C97-900989-8

FOR MY CHILDREN

CONTENTS